After Further Review

After Further Review

HOW REFLECTION AND ACTION WILL TURN YOUR SOMEDAYS INTO TODAY

◆ ◆ ◆

Joe Sweeney

Author of the *New York Times* bestseller
Networking Is a Contact Sport

Foreword by Lou Holtz

ISBN: 069289070X
ISBN-13: 9780692890707
Library of Congress Control Number: 2017907522
TriUnity Publications, Milwaukee, WI

Praise for *After Further Review*

◆ ◆ ◆

Getting the call right on the field is important; getting the call right in life is critical. *After Further Review* will help you to get the call right in life.

Bill Carollo—American football official

We have used the principles spelled out in *After Further Review* to help us grow professionally as well as in our personal lives.

Tom Sagissor—president, RBC Wealth Management

One of the challenges of sports is that we don't stop to reflect and analyze the consequences of our actions. *After Further Review* spells out a straightforward approach by using a unique analogy to the game of football and shows how the concepts apply to our everyday lives.

Craig Leipold—owner and governor, Minnesota Wild

After Further Review is a truly inspiring work that examines cultural, spiritual, and psychological barriers to engaging in reflection that will improve the quality and purpose of life. Joe writes from the heart about struggles with identity and fears of letting go.

Fr. Tony Zimmer—pastor, St. Anthony on the Lake

After Further Review will help you determine whether or not you're investing your life in the things that will produce the greatest meaning and joy.

Ed Wehmer—president/CEO, Wintrust Financial Corporation

After Further Review is a pep talk for anyone in the locker room of life about to head back out onto the playing field. It will challenge you, inspire you, and guide you on a journey toward the life you always wanted.

Lou Holtz—2008 College Football Hall of Fame class, author, speaker, broadcaster

What happens when you finally achieve what you've always wanted and discover it isn't everything it was cracked up to be? You read *After Further Review*.

Bob Harlan—chairman emeritus, Green Bay Packers

I've learned so much from Joe, both from his training sessions with us and through the strategies he shares in this book.

Jeff Gum—transitioning US Navy SEAL

Loved it! And so will anyone else who feels that the pressure and stress of everyday life have robbed them of the joy and sense of purpose they once knew.

Brian McCaskey—Vice President, Chicago Bears

Dedication

To Sr. Camille Kliebhan, OSF, PhD
Beloved teacher, spiritual mentor, and soulful friend

Acknowledgments

◆ ◆ ◆

THIS BOOK IS A COLLECTION of what I believe about life, religion, and spirituality communicated through the game of football.

It is my passion and new life goal that this book influence and help people to understand the complexities of life through a simple game called football.

Synchronicity connected me to Lyn Cryderman (collaborator on *A Purpose Driven Life*). Lyn helped to give form to all that was bubbling up inside of me. This book wouldn't be possible without his insights, ideas, and masterful crafting of the concepts and ideas.

Thank you to Colleen Heffron, my wingwoman, who helped make sure all the pieces fit together to make this possible.

Lisa Lunsford and Patrick O'Neill also gave their energy and insights to this book.

I am beyond grateful to Sr. Camille Kliebhan, Wayne Dyer, and Richard Rohr, as well as the other guides, mentors, and virtual board members who helped me to formulate this book.

Note to the Reader

◆ ◆ ◆

I'VE ALWAYS BEEN FASCINATED WITH what makes people tick—why they do what they do, believe what they believe. A few years ago, I began paying more attention to my own life—what gave me satisfaction, what made me happy, why I enjoyed some of my work and barely tolerated other aspects of my career. Along that journey, I began noticing that when I took the time to really reflect on my life, good things happened. I was able to sort out the things that really mattered and devote more of myself to those instead of chasing diversions that seemed important but never really delivered what I thought they would. It all came together a couple of years ago in what I describe in the second chapter as the absolute best year of my life. It was really amazing, and it got me wondering. Why can't everyone have a year like that? And why can't our next year be better than the last one? That's really what this book is all about—getting the most out of life, regardless of your finances, zip code, skin color, political party, religion, or gender.

Speaking of religion, you'll soon notice that I refer not only to my Catholic background, but also to wisdom figures and teachers from all ages. Whether or not you buy what they're selling, their words have been deeply inspirational to me. And to be perfectly honest, I need all the help I can get.

Because here's the deal: I'm no expert. I'm just an ordinary guy who took some time to look at how I was living, and based on those reviews, I made some changes. And while I still have days when I need to go back and read this book more than you do, overall I have more clarity, more purpose, more joy, even more fun. If it worked for a guy like me, I know it will work for you. You don't need any special formula, and I don't have a seven-step plan to turn your life around. All you need is a willingness to take an honest look at yourself and the courage to take a few baby steps toward the best you that you can ever be.

Contents

Foreword

◆ ◆ ◆

My GOOD FRIEND JOE SWEENEY has written a great book about the value of reflecting on what truly matters in life. And I can't for the life of me understand why he wants me to contribute something here, because for most of my career as a football coach and now a television broadcaster, you'd describe me as anything but reflective. As a coach, my job was to get my team ready to play on Saturday, and that left little time to do anything else but maybe eat and sleep.

After forty-four years of coaching—thirty-five as a head coach—I thought it was time to slow down a little, but that didn't last long. I soon began working as an analyst for Fox Sports. Like a lot of guys, I guess I just like staying busy. Just when I was about to tell Joe he needed to find someone else to comment on his book, I started reading it, and it really got my attention. Especially that part about the officials heading for the sidelines to review the previous play. I don't always like the results of those reviews, but I have to admit—it makes sense to stop, take a closer look, and make sure they made the right call.

That's what Joe's inviting us to do in this book, and when I think of it that way, I get it. I've found that looking more closely at how I live my life is really paying off. For one thing, it's helped me put things in perspective. For example, as proud as I am of a career that led to my being inducted into the football coaches' Hall of Fame, after further review, I've recognized how much greater it is to have my family, my faith, and the friendships that football has given me. When you're in the trenches—either on the sidelines during a big game or trying to meet a deadline at work—it's easy to think your job is all that matters. It's not, but I wouldn't have learned that without hitting the pause button to reflect on what matters.

You may not be in the NFL, but I'm pretty sure life for you is just as hectic. Trust me—better yet, trust Joe. Stopping regularly to take a closer look at how you're playing this bigger game will make the difference between the life you're currently living and the one you've always dreamed of.

Lou Holtz
2008 College Football Hall of Fame class, author, speaker, broadcaster

CHAPTER 1

Stop the Game—the Value of Reflection

◆ ◆ ◆

IF YOU'VE WATCHED AN NFL or college football game in the past decade, there's a good chance you've heard the phrase, "after further review." A minute or so before the official flips the switch on his microphone and utters those words, one of the coaches throws a red flag out onto the field, which is the coach's way of saying, "Hey, you just blew that call! Go take another look." You know what happens next. The game comes to a halt; the stadium gets quiet. Players from both teams head for the sidelines to grab water bottles and huddle around their coaches. The television announcers cut to a quick commercial or bring in their analysts to explain what's going on and maybe second-guess the outcome. Fans in the stands use the break in the action to head for the concession stands or maybe hit the restrooms. As all of this is going on, the guys in striped shirts head over to a corner of the field and do something that could change the entire outcome of the game.

With the help of his line judge, back judge, umpire, and other assistants both on the field and in the booth upstairs, the referee reviews the play from every possible angle captured by the many network-television cameras. He watches it in slow motion. He asks the broadcast crew to zoom in closer. To play it backward and forward. Because they want to get it right. Did the receiver catch the ball cleanly, or did it hit the ground first? Did the running back step out of bounds before he got into the end zone, or was it a valid touchdown? Was the quarterback's arm moving forward when the ball popped loose, or was he still winding up to throw?

Eventually, the referee peels off the headset that he used to communicate with the replay analyst and jogs toward the center of the field. Players and coaches turn their attention toward him while fans in the stadium or watching at home on TV stop what they're doing because they know what's coming. The official reaches to turn on his microphone and then says these words, **"After further review…"**

Football's a fast game, which is why even the most experienced officials will occasionally miss a call. With so much at stake—and with the advent of technology—the league decided in 1999 to initiate this break in the action to prevent any ill-informed calls from adversely affecting the outcome of the game. Stop the game. Review what just happened. Get clarity. Make a decision. Then resume play.

I love football. I love all sports, actually. When "my" team's playing and there's a stop in the action to allow the officials to review a play, I'm all eyes and ears. I want them to get it right. (OK—maybe I *really* want it to go my way, right or wrong.) But as much as I love football, it's just a game. When it comes to the much bigger game of life, shouldn't we be just as concerned about getting it right?

◆ ◆ ◆

We do not learn from experience…
we learn from reflecting on experience.
—John Dewey

A few years ago, one of the big insurance companies ran a commercial with the tagline "Life comes at you fast." I'll say. You may go to college, find a decent job, get married, buy a house, have kids, or enjoy exciting adventures. All that is great, but it takes a lot out of you and leaves little time to figure out if you're doing it all as well as you could. I used to think that pursuing all these good experiences gives you great "on-the-job" training about life. But as John Dewey once observed, "We do not learn from experience… we learn from reflecting on experience." A recent Harvard Business School study appears to support that. It found that reflecting on what you've done teaches you to do it better the next time. In fact, your performance improves when you focus on three key concepts:

1. Learning from experiences can be more effective if paired with reflection—that is, being intentional about pausing and reviewing the key lessons taught by experience.
2. Reflecting on what has been learned makes experience more productive.
3. Reflection builds confidence in an individual's ability to achieve goals, which in turn translates into higher learning and productivity.

This isn't just for business; it works in our personal lives as well. Taking the time to reflect on what's going on in your life will show you both the barriers to the fulfillment you desire as well as the strategies for overcoming those barriers.

But who has time to reflect?

We all do, but we seldom take the time to do it for at least a couple of reasons. It seems passive—feels like we're not doing anything, and most of us are hardwired for action. To some, it also feels a little New Agey, meaning a little out there. So unfortunately, it usually takes a crisis or other negative experience to force us into the "replay booth." At least, that's how it started for me. Even though things have gone pretty well for me, there have been times in my life when I wasn't content and knew I had to make a change. This once happened when I was frustrated with the company I was running. It was really a pretty good company, and I was working with some great people, but I just wasn't enjoying it. We'd close a deal, yet even though it meant more money for us, it didn't satisfy me like it once did. The thrill was definitely gone. I kept thinking, how can I reframe this to find more meaning? I can't just quit— I've got a mortgage to pay and college expenses coming up for our kids. I was a partner in the firm and still owned a percentage of the company. I wanted to try something different...something that really got my juices flowing, something that would allow me to make a real difference in people's lives.

I know I'm not alone here. I'm always running into people who seem to have it all together but who, in private moments, share similar feelings of frustration or discontent. The stories are different, but the themes are the same: "I always thought if I worked hard and achieved some success in life, I'd feel great. But I don't, and I don't know why." It's one of the big dilemmas of the good life, and even though our country has its problems, we all pretty much are living "the good life." It's just that so often it doesn't feel all that good.

My normal approach to those tough times was to double down and work harder. Just keep pushing yourself until you get to a better place...except you won't. You'll hit the proverbial wall, and that's how I began to learn the power of reflection. It was only through the process of reflecting on my life that I got the courage, insight, and wisdom to make some necessary changes.

That's why I previously hinted that if you want things to get better for you, don't try harder. Instead, do less. That's what reflection is all about: taking the time to look at what's really going on, examine it from every angle for more clarity, then make some decisions about what needs to change and how.

◆ ◆ ◆

Maybe your problems will not all disappear, but when you take time to reflect, you will see things about yourself you can't possibly notice when you're mired in the messy trenches of everyday life.

◆ ◆ ◆

Remember the Christmas classic, *It's a Wonderful Life*? I know, you probably weren't even born when it hit the big screen in 1946, but you have a TV, and like me, probably watch it at least once every December. It's set in Bedford Falls, New York, where Jimmy Stewart plays the despondent local banker, George Bailey. It's Christmas Eve, and George believes the Bailey Building and Loan Association, which he has spent his entire life helping to build and is vital to the townspeople of Bedford Falls, is on the verge of collapsing. To make matters worse, George thinks he's about to go to jail for bank fraud.

Lost in despair, he heads to the local bar, owned by his friend Giuseppe. After one too many drinks, George leaves the bar, crashes his car into a tree, and staggers to a bridge, apparently to take the big leap and end his life, only to be intercepted by Clarence, his guardian angel. Inspired by George's comment that he wished he had never been born, Clarence shows him how Bedford Falls would have turned out without him. The charming town has descended into grime and vice. Instead of delightful shops, cafes, and banks, pawn shops and sleazy nightclubs line the streets. In place of the affordable housing unit George helped build, there's an old cemetery. Most important, people whom George saved or nurtured are either ruined or gone.

By being forced to step back and look at his life from a distance, George realizes that he has...a wonderful life. Overcome with joy and emotion, he begs for the chance to live again. Clarence answers his prayer, and George runs home to be reunited with his family and discover that all of his problems have disappeared.

OK, maybe your problems will not all disappear, but when you take time to reflect, you will see things about yourself you can't possibly notice when you're mired in the messy trenches of everyday life. But just seeing isn't enough. The referees and officials look at the film and see what really happened on the field, but then they have to do something about it. Effective reflection always leads to action. Without acting on what you learn when you reflect on your life, it's just what we used to call navel-gazing: sitting around thinking deep thoughts but never doing anything about it. I love the way inspirational author and teacher Richard Rohr describes this: "If you spend your time only in contemplation without moving toward positive engagement, you end up with what many call spiritual constipation. I am afraid it is quite common."

Hmmm. Was he talking about Congress? But in all seriousness, the value of reflection lies not in what you learn, but in what you do about it. I think that's what even nonreligious people love about Jesus. He didn't just think up some nice things to say about the poor or the oppressed; he went out of his way to help them. If you spend some time reflecting on your life, I guarantee that you'll discover things that need to change. But then it's up to you to take that next step.

There's another benefit to reflection, one that may seem strange at first. After further review, reflection prepares you to die. As they say, the only constants in life are death and taxes. We're all gonna die, and for most people that's such a scary thought, we don't even entertain it. But as you reflect, you will begin to understand what's really important in life. Reflection creates detachment, which is incredibly freeing. You are no longer attached to things that you feel you can't live without but weigh you down and hold you back, things like status (the car you drive, the club you belong to), power (title, position, job), or conformity (fitting into a particular label). Those things used to have an incredible influence on me—but no longer do. If I reflect and an idea pops into my head that seems offbeat or even a little crazy, I take it pretty seriously, and more often than not, I give it a try. Why not? Why live your life trying to conform to other people's opinions of you?

Imagine what you might do, where you might go, or who you might inspire if you felt completely detached from the stuff in your life that's holding you back. That's what reflection offers. The ultimate reflection leads to "deathbed decisions." You will begin to contemplate looming choices as if you are on your deathbed.

And it's not that complex. Set aside some time on your calendar to deliberately find a quiet place with few distractions. Give yourself at least thirty minutes—an hour would be better. When the appointed time arrives, grab a notebook or tablet and sit quietly, clearing your mind. I've found that it helps to create rituals—pour yourself a cup of tea or coffee, read from a spiritual book or sacred text, close your eyes, mentally remove all labels attached to your life, and listen past the noise in your life for the sounds of nature. Some people enter into a more reflective state with the help of quiet, soothing music in the background. We're all different, so you may need to experiment at first, but the goal is always the same—to enter a time and space where there are as few distractions as possible so that you are open to whatever comes into your mind.

◆ ◆ ◆

Reflection creates detachment, which is incredibly freeing.

◆ ◆ ◆

In my book *Moving the Needle,* I wrote that if you want to get clear, get quiet. There's magic and power in the art of reflection—power to inspire you to do something beyond your wildest dreams. You will find a reason for living that is bigger than yourself that will transform the way you work and live and eventually enable you to change the world.

In professional baseball, the journey from the minor leagues to the majors is often long and circuitous. You bounce around the country, playing in small ballparks and eating a lot of fast food. The goal is to give you some valuable experience and prepare you for the next level. If you pay attention and put in the necessary work, you will one day get that call.

I think that's about to happen to you.

Go to the Tape

1. Over the course of a week, approximately how much time do you spend reflecting on your life?

2. Identify three places where you can be alone, get energized, and not be interrupted (a park, private study, house of worship, bookstore, gym, and so on).
3. Outside of your career, what would you like to accomplish?
4. What are some calls you missed—mistakes you've made—and what do you think led to those missed calls?
5. Does the idea of spending one hour alone without an agenda excite you, scare you, or seem ridiculous to you? Explain.

CHAPTER 2

Transform Your Life

◆ ◆ ◆

I THINK I KNOW YOU. No, we've never met, but I'm pretty sure I understand where you are in life right now. You graduated from college about a dozen or more years ago, and after a few false starts you've landed a pretty good position with a pretty good company. Or maybe you pulled together some money and maxed out a couple of credit cards to start your own business. Doesn't matter, because now you're exhausted. And a little bored. You're making a whole lot more money than you did when you were getting started, but you still worry about money. Back when you were making the big jump from an apartment to a bungalow and dreaming about today, life seemed a lot more fun. Or exciting. Or something. But now, that something—whatever it is—is missing.

◆ ◆ ◆

Why the nagging feeling that the life you
always thought you wanted isn't quite
delivering what you expected?

◆ ◆ ◆

How do I know this about you? Because this pattern is so common for men and women in our culture today. You do everything you're supposed to do, and at some point you sort of hit a wall. Previous generations called it a midlife crisis, but that's not quite it, right? You're not thinking about buying a Harley and leaving your upper-middle-class life in search of adventure. You may already own a Harley, and besides, it's not like your life is a mess. In fact, it's pretty good. Your kids are about to head off on their own or maybe have already left the nest, and despite all your mistakes, they've turned out better than you expected. Your dream job is starting to lose its shine, but it's far from being a nightmare. You've got plenty of tread left and see a lot of good things down the road. So why the nagging feeling that the life you always thought you wanted isn't quite delivering what you expected?

At least that's how I felt.

I grew up in a great family. Irish Catholic. The ninth boy out of ten kids. I was taught by my dad's example that if you worked hard and stayed out of trouble, you'd be rewarded with a good life. And he was right. I worked my way through college, got a decent job, and built a few companies, including one that let me live the dream as a sports agent. Can you imagine what it's like to be a lifelong jock and watch an NFL game from the sidelines? Or an NHL game from a luxury suite—then hang out with the team in the locker room after the game? Can it get any better than that?

Apparently it can, because despite all my perceived "dream life," it wasn't enough. I was always in a hurry. I never had enough time. Never had enough money. Yeah, I built some companies, but I also made my share of stupid decisions. Listen, I've made my share of mistakes. In fact, I could probably write an entire book on all the mistakes I've made.

A few years ago, I found myself in line for my all-time dream job—and I didn't get it. They gave it to someone else, and I was pretty bummed out. I once again had bought into the idea that if I just got that _____ (fill in the blank), I'd finally be happy.

You'd think I would have learned by then, but I hadn't. I eventually got over my disappointment and jumped right back into the fray that we call the good life.

I should have been content with the life I had because it really was pretty good, but I was always driven for more. I fell into the trap of comparing myself with my friends. Unfortunately, I had a lot of really rich and successful friends, so I never measured up, which only drove me to try harder and take more risks. You've heard the old adage, "You can't keep up with the Joneses." Well, I learned that even if you finally catch up to them, they refinance, and you're screwed!

People who think they know me are going to read this and wonder, "Who is Sweeney talking about?" Because on the outside, I was the portrait of the American dream. Joe's got it all. A nice family and four well-adjusted kids. Everyone in town knows the Sweeneys. We're heavily involved in the community. Live in a nice house in a coveted neighborhood. Investment banker. Former sports agent. Well connected. Serving on several boards. Always happy, upbeat. But inside, I was just another insecure American male (some people say that's redundant). I thought having a lot of things would fulfill me—that if I drove a Lexus 460LS then I'd be satisfied or that by owning a five-bedroom home with a pool by the lake I'd be happy.

◆ ◆ ◆

Are you trying to keep up with the Joneses?
Even if you finally catch up to them, they refinance,
and you're screwed!

◆ ◆ ◆

Maybe that works for you, but all that stuff about the good life was what the Bible called "dung," and honest biblical scholars will admit that's the cleaned-up version, as the good apostle likely called it bullshit.

I did all the right things, but instead of feeling fulfilled or at peace, I occasionally wrestled with a smoldering discontent. Nothing pathological—I wasn't an alcoholic. My life wasn't falling apart. And even though I made some lousy financial decisions, I wasn't broke. It's just that life for me wasn't delivering what I thought it would, but I had no clue what to do about it. That smoldering discontent manifested itself in things like boredom, frustration, and anxiety, which was crazy because in so many ways I was living the dream.

And then I started getting quiet and reflecting on my life, taking the time to focus on things that really mattered. I tried looking inside as much as I looked outside. It didn't happen overnight, but eventually I began to "get it." I'm still learning, but after further review of my life, I began to see what was really going on and began reversing the calls I once thought were right.

Which brings me to last year—the best year of my life (so far).

As I look back on it, I almost have to pinch myself. For example, in January I left the investment-banking firm that I was running to explore opportunities to do things that really mattered, things that made a difference. I must give credit here to a friend who encouraged me to attend a retreat, which helped clarify for me what those opportunities would look like. At the same time, I needed an income, but surprisingly, I wasn't anxious about finances, which for me was a real departure. I used to worry about money all the time, but here I was, unemployed (sort of), and not the least bit concerned. And by the end of the month, I was offered a lucrative board position and secured enough speaking engagements to keep me afloat for the year.

In February, the navy SEALs hired me to study how they train their guys and then make recommendations based on my experiences in the business and sports worlds. One of the perks of this assignment was joining thirty-seven SEALs and eight of their instructors on San Clemente Island for four days. What a blast, literally. Remember, I'm a guy. Guys love things that go *bang*. For four days I got to hang out with the military's finest and blow things up. If that wasn't enough, I got to swim with the SEALs and teach their leadership team about life lessons. What's not to love about that? I'm also a Catholic who's trying to dig deeper into the world of faith and belief, so when I was asked to speak to a group of six hundred young students and parents at our diocesan confirmation preparation, I couldn't believe it. What an honor to be able to influence the next generation of world changers.

I never used to have enough time for the things in life that truly mattered, but gradually I have made time to do more things with my family, including an awesome reunion with my siblings and all the kids. In March, I went to a retreat featuring one of my heroes, Ken Blanchard, author of several books, including the best-selling *One-Minute Manager*. Then a mentor and a key influencer in my life invited me to mentor evangelical church leaders at a two-day retreat. I cleaned up my language and tried not to cross myself too many times. We had a great time, and this experience really began to influence my values and beliefs. In fact, I have to give credit to my coaches, Lloyd Reeb and Dick Gygi, for helping to guide me on my journey.

In April, I was invited back to teach the navy SEALs who were about to transition back into civilian society. These guys are awesome, and just to be around them is an inspiration. While I was there, they let me join them in a live-action Maritime Interdiction Operation—or MIO. How cool, I thought. I'm going to actually engage in combat exercises like a real navy SEAL. Remember how Capt. Richard Phillips's freighter was boarded by Somali pirates, and then a SEAL team rescued him and the crew? That's an MIO, and my assignment was to play Captain Phillips. Six different times. Three daytime operations and three at night. I spent part of the time flat on my face with a SEAL's boot on my neck and a gun barrel inches away from my head. Then when they let me up, it was only to interrogate me, and even though this wasn't for real, tell that to the SEALs. Let's just say I was ready to spill all my secrets. Do I still think this was a great year? You bet!

Throughout the year, I kept getting to do what I love so much, and that's speaking to groups, both corporate and nonprofit. But I'm not a motivational speaker. I hate that crap. Motivation is trying to get people to do something they don't want to do. So you end up with a lot of miserable people doing a better job of what they hate doing. I prefer to *inspire* people to do what they wish they could do but never dreamed they would be able to do.

In June, I traveled with the navy SEALs to Normandy. It still sends chills up my spine as I recall walking the beach where more than two hundred thousand Allied soldiers paid the ultimate price for our freedom. The term "life-changing" is overused, but this was a truly life-changing experience. Every evening in the village of Sainte-Mère-Église, I got to hang out with members of "the greatest generation"—former warriors with the 101st and 82nd airborne divisions who actually jumped in on D Day—I never drank so much beer or cried so much in my life as I did that week listening to these guys tell their stories and share their disdain for Hitler. Then I spent a few days in Paris, which was like icing on an already delicious cake.

By this time, I'm asking myself, "What is going on?" I'm waiting for the proverbial shoe to drop. Every month seems to bring new opportunities to experience life as I always thought it was meant to be.

It gets better. In July, I spoke to a university class in Rome, then spent two weeks in Italy that included dinner with Cardinal Harvey, the archpriest of Saint Paul's, who served as prefect to the papal household of Popes John Paul II and Benedict XVI. After the visit to the Vatican, I went to Assisi and traced the steps of my favorite saint, Saint Francis. Then I was given several experiences that for a basketball junkie like me were beyond awesome. First, I was asked to speak to the University of Wisconsin men's basketball team at the beginning of the season by a former client and friend, Coach Bo Ryan, to help the team move the needle and get back to the Final Four. Then I was lucky enough to watch them in person in the national championship game in Indianapolis against Duke.

Coach Steve Wojciechowski invited me to work with his Marquette men's basketball team on developing life skills for his players during their season. And yes, in case you are wondering, when Wisconsin and Marquette faced off against each other that season, I was praying for a tie.

If all this wasn't enough, Peter Feigin, president of the Milwaukee Bucks, asked me to speak to his two hundred employees and sales staff on networking and business development. For a guy as into sports as I am, this was about as good as it gets.

I could go on and on, but I read what I just wrote and thought, "Who is this?" Let's just say that in addition to the ordinary ups and downs we all have, a lot of good things were happening to me. And it wasn't all fun and games. For example, I signed up for a Jesuit silent retreat. If you know anything about the Jesuits, you know that these are hard-core dudes who are serious about their faith. When they offer a silent retreat, it's silent. As in you don't talk, except when you go to the conferences where the priest gives a talk. That's right. The guy who loves to talk finds himself tucked away at a retreat house with nothing but my thoughts. There was a time when I would have preferred walking barefoot on broken glass to attending a silent retreat. People had tried for twenty-five years to drag me off to one, but I thought it was silly. Yet this may have been the most transformative experience of my life. This is going to sound weird, but one day, while lying on my mattress in my sparse room, I watched a spider for several minutes. I don't even like spiders—probably have seen hundreds of them in my life yet without *really* seeing them. But this retreat slowed me down, allowing me to see all of life more clearly than ever before. It was so unbelievably impactful that I made the commitment right then and there: I'm going to attend a silent retreat every year until I leave this earth. Oh, that's another thing. I'm no longer afraid of death. In fact, if I die in the near future, I'm pretty good to go.

◆ ◆ ◆

I started getting quiet and reflecting on my life, taking the time to focus on things that really mattered.

◆ ◆ ◆

Here's the best part of the greatest year of my life. I feel like I have eliminated my FOMO (fear-of-missing-out) syndrome—even when things don't turn out the way I wish they would, because you-know-what still happens. Where I used to try to keep up with others, I realize now that I'm not trying to be better than anyone else; I'm just trying to be better than I used to be. But my best year ever is a lot more than just getting to go on fun adventures. We all get to do fun activities in life. What made it so great is that the smoldering discontent has been transformed into positive energy that gives my life more meaning and clarity. I have a clearer sense of purpose. I care less about my needs and find great joy in helping others. In fact, that's become my mission in life. The guy who couldn't get enough now can't give himself away enough.

And that's what this book is all about. I can say I think I know you because I'm convinced that men and women who've lived a few years in our culture struggle with the same smoldering discontent I have experienced. I finally got sick of it and began a journey of discovery that I want to share with you. It's not a magic formula or a guarantee of success. It won't happen overnight, but it can begin today. Instead of asking you to do more, I'm going to challenge you to do less. In fact, that's a good place to start.

Close the book, set it down, push your recliner back, and describe the best moment of your day, week, or month. Now reflect on it for a few minutes. Look at that moment from every angle. Replay it from someone else's perspective.

After further review, what really happened?

Go to the Tape

1. Describe the best year of your life. What made it so great? What did you learn from it?
2. Describe the worst year of your life. What stands out that made it so bad?
3. How satisfied are you with the way your life is going?
4. What excites you or leaves you feeling on top of the world?
5. What don't people know about you that would surprise them?

6. What wakes you up at night and won't let you get back to sleep?
7. If you could create a do-over in one area of your life, what would it be?

CHAPTER 3

You're Being Called Up—You Belong to Something Bigger than Yourself

◆ ◆ ◆

True heroism is remarkably sober, very undramatic.
It is not the urge to surpass all others at whatever the
cost, but the urge to serve others whatever the cost.

—ARTHUR ASHE

WE'VE ALL SEEN IT HAPPEN, even recently. A rookie comes into the league who thinks he's God's gift to the NFL. Then he sustains a head injury—as in, his head gets huge. The reason why his helmet is suddenly too small is that he started believing all those things the sports writers wrote about him, and now even his teammates are sick of him. He becomes a distraction on and off the field, and it isn't long before he moves on to another team or drops completely off the face of the NFL. I think you know what I'm talking about. Throughout my years in sports management, I saw it happen a lot, and it wasn't pretty. Both the team and the star suffered from his inflated ego.

You see, in the world of sports, no one is bigger than the team or the game. It doesn't matter if you're the highest-paid player, the coach, the equipment manager, or a young intern helping to keep stats as a way to try to get into the sports business; each has a role to play that contributes to the overall success of the team. If you are part of the team, you are important, and if you don't believe it, consider what goes on in the operating rooms of hospitals in America. The surgeon is the star quarterback, and without him or her, whoever's lying on the operating table is in trouble. But it's the nurses and technicians and other highly trained teammates who help the surgeon fix whatever's broken in that patient. But even if the surgeon and those other medical professionals do their jobs well, the outcome is still not certain. Last year, 2.5 million people got infections from operating rooms, which means the people who clean the operating room are just as important as the doc who performs the surgery. If you're here and part of the team, you're important. If you're here and not part of the team, maybe you're in the wrong place.

Too often, we think we're the only ones who matter; we're all pretty vulnerable to believing everything revolves around us. It's called narcissism, a word that originated from Narcissus, the character in Greek mythology who fell in love with his own image reflected in a pool of water. According to psychologists Jean M. Twenge and W. Keith Campbell, the United States is currently experiencing an epidemic of narcissism.

We're falling in love with ourselves!

One of the first things that happens when you pause to reflect is that you realize Copernicus was right: you're not the center of the universe. It's not all about you. But unless you pause the game and look at the replay of your life, you'll never understand that;

every message in our culture says just the opposite. Consider some of these gems from advertising:

* "You Rule" (Virgin Mobile)
* "Have It Your Way" (Burger King)
* "Enough about us. Let's talk about you." (Lincoln MKX)
* "You Deserve Better" (Rocket Mortgage/Quicken Loans)
* "TV the Way You Want It" (Amazon Fire TV)
* "Begin Your Own Tradition" (Patek Philippe)
* "Air travel engineered around you." (Lufthansa)
* "Work the way you want." (Dropbox Business)
* "I Am What I Am" (Reebok)
* "Because You're Worth It" (L'Oréal)
* "My Life. My Card." (American Express)

Advertisers understand how much we love ourselves and have learned how to use that narcissism to sell us items we don't need. "That person you love so much is not complete until you buy our product." I find it ironic that "branding" has become the buzzword in the marketing world. Do you know how branding really got started? Not with Nike, Coke, or Starbucks—all great brands recognized the world over. Branding originated with cows and slaves who were literally branded with a hot iron to imprint the owner's symbol into their flesh. Branding represented ownership. While branding can be positive—great brands are usually the result of a company working hard to earn a great reputation—it can also mislead you into thinking you matter way more than you do. When a brand's message tells you that you need it in order to be cool, loved, or accepted—in order to be complete as a human being—you'll do whatever it asks of you. Cultural stereotypes always inhibit your ability to hear your calling.

What a crazy way to live, but we've all done it, right?

Then there's the whole social-media craze, which we think connects us—and to an extent it does—but it does so by practically screaming, "Look at me! Look at me!" We post carefully edited pictures on Facebook of our kids to draw attention to our perfect families (ever seen a photo of Dad shuffling around the living room in his boxers or Mom without her makeup?) And those profiles we create about ourselves? Well—you're good, but not *that* good. Between posts on Facebook, we Twitter away about the most mundane details of our lives because, of course, the whole world wants to know that we just finished taking out the garbage. Then there's my favorite: taking a picture with your cell phone of your meal at that fancy restaurant and texting it to your friends, essentially saying, "Look at me eating at a nice restaurant while you're having leftovers." Seriously? OK, I've done it, too. And don't get me wrong—I'm on Facebook, I try to manage a Twitter account, and I've hired marketing teams to get the word out about my books. We all like to share the good things in our lives with others, but for many, it's gotten way out of hand. Did you know you can hire fake paparazzi to follow you around and snap pictures so that you appear to be somebody important?

You know what I *really* think about social media, though? It reveals how desperately we want to belong to something bigger than ourselves. The American Psychological Association recently published a report about how social media is one of the major factors in contemporary adult anxiety.

In fact, more than seventy years ago, a psychologist named Abraham Maslow studied some of the most successful people in the world, including Albert Einstein, Eleanor Roosevelt, and Frederick Douglass. He included in his study the top 1 percent of the total college population in the United States. From that expansive study, which became known as "Maslow's Hierarchy of Needs," he concluded that aside from our functional physiological needs and the need for safety, one of our greatest needs as humans is to belong. It's firmly embedded in our emotional and spiritual DNA.

Why else would fifty-seven-year-old men paint their faces yellow and green, drive to Green Bay, Wisconsin, and brave minus-ten-degree weather for three hours? It's all about one thing: belonging. They endure all that and more so that they can belong to Packer Nation. As they shiver in the cold or bake in the sun or get drenched by monsoon-like rain, they get swept up in something far greater than themselves. They are not individual sports fans but are part of a movement—a family—joining together to cheer their team. And trust me, whether it's the eighty thousand fans packed into a home game at Lambeau Field or one of the tens of millions cheeseheads worldwide, we take belonging pretty seriously. I know I'm biased, having been born and raised in Wisconsin, but Packer fans are the most dedicated sports fans in the world (sorry, Chicago). In fact, the Packers are the only team in the NFL that are literally *owned* by the fans. We buy stock in the team and proudly display the stock certificates (which are of no real value) in our green-and-gold-painted basements. Because of this phenomenon, the Green Bay Packers is the only team in the NFL that can never be moved to another city. Some 250,000 team owners spread all across the country would never let that happen!

I guess I got a little carried away there, but that's what happens when you get over yourself and join something bigger, and the only way you can do that is by hitting the pause button and spending some time reflecting. When you begin deliberately doing that, you will soon break free from the tyranny of narcissism, which compels you to worry about what you have or don't have and how you stack up against others.

◆ ◆ ◆

When they discover the center of the universe, a lot of people will be disappointed to discover they are not it.
—Bernard C. Bailey

◆ ◆ ◆

When I began reflecting on my life, I saw how I was making the mistake of buying into the myth that I was defined by what I owned or what I did. I had been blessed with a lot of nice things and had the kind of career that many would envy. But a nice lifestyle and enviable career weren't doing much for me. It certainly didn't make me feel fulfilled or satisfied. In fact, the more I had, the more I wanted. It was only as I began pausing to honestly examine my life that I was able to see that what my soul really craved could be satisfied only by something bigger—something that is not tethered to money, status, or recognition. For me, raised in the Catholic tradition, that "something bigger" is God. But it's more than just a recognition that He's out there somewhere in the cosmos. To benefit from it, I need to tap into it and remain connected, which I do through prayer, worship, and meditation. In fact, reflection for me is really listening to the still, small voice of God. I resonate with the French mathematician Blaise Pascal, who wrote in the seventeenth century:

What else does this craving, and this helplessness, proclaim but that there was once in man a true happiness, of which all that now remains is the empty print and trace? This he tries in vain to fill with everything around him, seeking in things that are not there the help he cannot find in those that are, though none can help, since this infinite abyss can be filled only with an infinite and immutable object; in other words, by God himself.

That works for me, but it doesn't have to for you. You may be more comfortable thinking in terms of a higher power, the universe, the divine mind, or energy. C. S. Lewis wrote about the *numinous,* or, as he described it, the sense that "there is a mighty spirit in the room...This feeling may be described as awe, and the object which excites it is the Numinous." Martin Buber writes that human life finds meaning in relationships, and the highest, most fulfilling re-lationship is what he calls the "I-thou," which ultimately connects us to God. What Buber is talking about is that when we connect with something bigger, we realize we are called, and when we are called it suggests there must be a caller. After further review, the question that comes to mind is "Who's doing the calling?" We come to the realization that it is our creator. Staying connected cre-ates clarity, whereas isolation contributes to confusion.

Even people who are not religious sense something beyond themselves when they see a beautiful sunset or hear the ocean surf rhythmically pounding the shore. It's that feeling I believe we all have that there's something out there that has the capacity to inspire us, to lift us beyond ourselves. A friend recently sent me a link to a video that captures this sense of our smallness compared to the vast-ness of whatever you want to call your "something bigger." It begins with the frame filled with a close-up of the human eye, and as the camera backs away, we see that it belongs to a lovely young woman. But the camera keeps rising until we see the outline of the United States, and then planet earth, our solar system, and it just keeps on rising higher and deeper into the universe, passing through galaxies all the way out to ten billion light-years. But then it zooms back down to that girl lying on her back; only this time it continues into her pupil, taking us through her retina, into a blood vessel, passing through blood cells, then chromosomes, past the microscopic 10-nm fiber, individual atoms, electrons, and into the tiniest entity of human matter. It's amazing, even emotional, because it demonstrates the awesome relationship between each of us and "the other."

Now here's the really cool part of all of this. Call it God, a higher power, energy, or whatever—there's nothing you have to do to connect to this power. By virtue of being human, you're already connected. It's right there in front of you. But just like in a football game when the ref claims the wide receiver did not have both feet in bounds when he caught the ball, we have to review our lives through reflection to see more clearly what's really going on. After further review, you realize you're not the center of the universe, but it's OK because you're connected!

Something else happens when you pause to look inside yourself. That force field of energy is calling you to a deeper purpose, a divine assignment designed for your unique gifts, skills, and personality. At first, it will be a quiet whisper, barely audible. In fact, that gentle voice has been there all along, calling you to a much greater adventure than you could ever imagine. But you couldn't hear it. You were too busy. Too important. We think we've got it all figured out, but we really don't. Or we're just too absorbed with ourselves to care, which is why that voice persists. If you ignore it, the whisper will build to a scream, a crippling addiction, a crisis, or a loss. Sadly, it often takes such uncomfortable events to get our attention. How much better to carve out time and space to reflect, to listen, to hear that whisper. When you hear that voice clearly, its words will be at once beautifully appealing and scary as hell. That's OK. It took me a while to find my stride and become comfortable with the new direction to which I was being called. To be honest, I was worried that people would think I was crazy for making changes at this stage of the game.

As you listen to that voice calling you to something beyond your wildest dreams and begin to act on it, you'll have days when you second-guess yourself. When that happens, you have a choice. You can retreat, mull over past accomplishments, and maybe step back into the past. Or you can define who you are by what you're doing *right now*. In fact, those periods of doubt will be transformational because they make you face your weaknesses, your limitations, and your past. They force you to define yourself not by where you've been but by where you're going. When you face that discomfort and uncertainty and forge ahead anyway, it strengthens you as a person, opening doors to a better you. As Joseph Campbell wrote in *The Hero's Journey*, "When you feel the nudge you have to face it and listen to it."

◆ ◆ ◆

That force field of energy is calling you to a deeper purpose, a divine assignment designed for your unique gifts, skills, and personality.

◆ ◆ ◆

I have a friend who, for the past eight years, has worked for the campus ministry department at a Jesuit college. She lives in a freshman residence hall and serves as a mentor to the students in the hall. She told me that she tries to encourage students to stop and reflect because then they will learn to hear God's voice. To get you started, here are some of the things I've adapted from her efforts to help her students slow down and listen:

* Sit in a dark room with calm, relaxing music (perhaps great worship music) playing softly.
* Focus on different muscles, flex them, and then relax them, releasing tension.
* Reflect on the day and think about what you are thankful for.
* Think about the emotions you experienced today.
* Look back on how you responded to people and events.
* Try to identify any "God winks" you might have had, which are experiences during which you felt God or a powerful positive force present.

Of course, you may have other ways to reflect, but what's important is that you begin by calming your body before you calm the mind. If you fail to do that, your mind will likely continue to race as you think about all the items on your to-do list, the depressing event you heard on the news, or the football game you just watched. Or to put it another way, we are both spirit and body. We cannot just command our minds to reflect on cue. In fact, to reflect effectively, we may need to let go of our attachment to the goal of reflecting and begin by simply being present in our bodies, breathing slowly and deeply until both mind and body are calm.

I can't tell you what your assignment will be, though I believe the highest calling for any of us is to serve others in some capacity. But I can assure you that if you regularly set aside time to sit quietly and reflect on your life, you will eventually know with clarity what it is you are called to do. The key is to start with small amounts of time and build up to more. Then it will be up to you. A lot of people think they're in the game, but they're really just watching from the stands. If you want to get out of the stands and run out onto the field, find your calling, and then—even if it seems scary, even if you're afraid you'll fail—go for it. And when the going gets tough, remember these words from Theodore Roosevelt:

It is not the critic who counts; not the man who points out how the strong man stumbles, or whether the doer of deeds could have done them better. The credit belongs to the man who is actually in the arena, whose face is marred by dust and sweat and blood; who strives valiantly; who errs, who comes up short again and again, because there is no effort without error or shortcoming; but who does actually strive to do the deeds; who knows great enthusiasms, the great devotions; who spends himself in a worthy cause; who at the best knows in the end the triumph of high achievement, and who at the worst, if he fails, at least fails while daring greatly, so that his place shall never be with those cold and timid souls who neither know victory nor defeat.

◆ ◆ ◆

If you knew who was walking through you at all times...all angst, anxiety and doubt would be eliminated from your life because you would know you are living a life bigger than yourself.
—Helen Schulman, *Course in Miracles*

The spiritual journey leads you to the day when you realize someone is living in and through you, and you are part of a greater mystery. Richard Rohr talks about a three-step process:

1. Start connecting better to other people, animals, and nature.
2. Grow deeper and more meaningful relationships with people.
3. Then you will experience full connectedness and union with our creator.

Helen Schulman writes in *Course in Miracles*, "If you knew who was walking through you at all times…all angst, anxiety and doubt would be eliminated from your life because you would know you are living a life bigger than yourself."

Go to the Tape

1. In what ways are you affected by a "culture of narcissism"?
2. What are you most excited about in your life?
3. What matters most to you in life? Does it match up with what you are doing? If you say your family is most important, and you are working one hundred hours per week—this doesn't match.
4. What do you tend to think about as you fall asleep at night?
5. If you had no job, title, or reputation to protect, would you be the same person you are right now? Explain.
6. Narcissus looked into a pool of water, saw his reflection, and fell in love with himself. What do you see when you look in the mirror?
7. What do you consider your purpose in life to be?

CHAPTER 4

Game Plan—Where Are You Going?

◆ ◆ ◆

Clarity of purpose is inspirational.

—Marcus Luttrell, *Lone Survivor*

I REMEMBER PLAYING TOUCH FOOTBALL with my brothers and neighborhood kids. First of all, "touch" is a relative term in backyard football. As in, whenever I carried the ball, I always ended up on my backside. Still, it was great fun, those chilly autumn Saturdays when each of us pretended to be one of our gridiron heroes. "Bart Starr" would call us into the huddle, diagram a play on the palm of his hand, and then we'd line up and try to figure out where to run or who to block. Just like in the NFL, right?

Not exactly.

Our backyard quarterbacks had maybe three plays in their arsenal: go long, go deep, or end around. Most NFL teams have more than one thousand plays at their disposal. We developed our "strategy" in each of those huddles, kneeling on the withered grass as the QB told us what to do. In the NFL, almost as soon as one game ends, the coaches begin working on one of the most important aspects of the sport: the game plan. You've heard about the long hours put in by NFL coaches? It's true. They often don't leave the training facilities until late at night, and most of that time is spent developing and fine-tuning the plan that will prepare them for the next game.

They start by watching tapes of their opponent, looking for strengths to prepare for and weaknesses to exploit. The offensive coordinator might meet with the quarterback and get his input. For example, they may be facing a defense that likes to go with the 4–3 most of the time, so coach and QB will look through their playbook for plays that are designed to work best against the 4–3. The coaches also look at their assets—their players—and adjust the game plan based on who's starting the next game. They might have a couple of rookies and a backup center on the offensive line, so they'll limit the number of formations and plays so that these untested players don't get confused. Throughout the week, coaches and key players will continue to fine-tune the game plan until around the Friday before a Sunday game, when they go over the game plan with the entire team, then break into position units and drill down on it even further.

Why all this fuss over the game plan? Why not just wing it like we did? Because a lot's at stake. A chance to win your division. Make the playoffs. The Super Bowl. Bigger payday. Maybe setting yourself up for Hall of Fame consideration.

So if a football team puts that kind of time and effort into a plan for a *game,* doesn't it make sense that each of us would be just as willing to develop a plan for our *lives*?

◆ ◆ ◆

Most of us just sort of float through our
lives without thinking much about where
we're going or what we want to achieve.

◆ ◆ ◆

It's not like we're clueless about planning. If you work in any kind of business environment, you've probably seen or even helped develop your company's strategic plan. When it's vacation time, you probably sit down and map out your plans so that you'll pack as much fun and relaxation into your getaway as possible. If you're handy with tools, you wouldn't think of building or making something without a plan. Yet most of us just sort of float through our lives without thinking much about where we're going or what we want to achieve. And that's really what a game plan—for the NFL or your life—is all about: determining what you want to accomplish and then identifying how you're going to accomplish it.

The late Peter Drucker, known as the father of modern management, once noted that "nothing good happens by accident." I totally agree. I've always been a planner, even in my younger years, when a lot of people don't think much about the future. I set aside money for our kids' college bills and tried to contribute to an IRA. As a businessman, I knew the value of both short- and long-range planning. But where many of us fall short is when it comes to how we live our personal lives, which is to say we tend to spend little time thinking about things like purpose and meaning. Like most people on the front end of their careers, I lived pretty much for the present when it came to those things. But when I began reflecting on my life, it became pretty clear to me that I needed to pay as much attention to my life goals and mission as I did to my business or financial goals if I wanted to live the kind of life that would leave me with no regrets on my deathbed.

So why are we so reluctant to develop a game plan for our lives? I think one reason is that we think having a plan will restrict us. We like our freedom, and if we have to stick to a plan, we'll miss out on all those good things that are just waiting to fall into our laps. So…how's that working for you?

Spontaneity may sound appealing, but you'll actually experience more freedom if you live according to a plan. The late, great football coach, Vince Lombardi, was deeply influenced by his education at Jesuit schools. Among other things, Jesuits place a great emphasis on helping others understand their purpose in life, which according to them is to glorify God through serving others. It is from this teaching that Coach Lombardi coined the phrase, "freedom through discipline." The Jesuits live highly disciplined lives, which enables them to do great things for others. Likewise, Lombardi believed that by teaching and emphasizing discipline to his players, they would best be able to make the right decisions and execute plays to the best of their abilities. In a sense, it is through discipline, normally thought of as being restrictive, that his players were free to play to and beyond their potential. He taught them to identify and cultivate their talents so that they could achieve their goals of becoming the best players they could possibly be. He frequently reminded his players, "I don't want you to be anyone else but you. But I need you to be the best version of who you are."

That's what living your life according to a plan will do. It will enable you to become the best version of who you are. But I'd like you to take it a step further. What about your family? I hate to admit this, but it wasn't until recently that I focused my attention on creating a plan—with their input—for our family. Your personal life and that of your family is far too important to let it run on autopilot. No football team or business would consider operating without a plan, and you shouldn't, either.

◆ ◆ ◆

Spontaneity may sound appealing, but you'll actually experience more freedom if you live according to a plan.

◆ ◆ ◆

So how do you actually do it? I like to use the example of the global positioning service, or GPS. Basically, a GPS does three things: it tells you where you are, shows you your destination, and most importantly, it shows you the best route to get where you want to go. Using the GPS model, ask yourself these three questions:

✦ Where are you in your personal life? Your relationships? Your relationship, if any, to a higher power?
✦ Where would you like to be—in what areas do you want to grow—over the next twelve months, one to five years, and five years and beyond?
✦ What steps do you need to take to grow in those areas?

It's not rocket science, but for some reason, we seldom spend much time on questions like these for ourselves or our families. We spend more time planning our vacations than we do our lives. I've gotten a lot of help from my friends at the Halftime Institute (the leading authority on creating a second half defined by joy, impact, and balance) with this type of personal planning, and they have shared one concept that really resonates with me and prompts the question, "What would your life look like if it really turned out great?" Now, none of us will ever be perfect, but this question is a great way to describe the place you would like to be—the destination on your life's GPS. That question led me to drill down on my values, my dreams, and the things that were really important to me. Unfortunately, like so many guys trying to do all the right things, I wasn't always clear on what those "right things" were. According to Dynamic Catholic founder Matthew Kelly, "What we have done as a society is take the really important things and trivialized them, and we've taken some trivial things and made them really important."

Over time I began putting together a game plan that covered three areas: determining the values I want to live by, building a thriving family, and getting closer to my kids. These were the areas that were now important to me after reflecting on my life—the destination I punched in on my life's GPS. Here's what I came up with on life values:

- *Faith.* Live the prayer of Saint Francis: recite daily.
- *Family.* Practice thriving family.
- *Health.* I am FLA (I feel fit, lean, and alive when my weight is at 175 pounds).
- *Generosity.* Start with giving: give more than I take.
- *Servanthood.* Golden Rule: do unto others. Leave everything better than how you found it. People, places, and events.

It's one thing to write values like this down, but we get so distracted and off course—at least I do—so I printed this list on some business cards, laminated them, and put one in my wallet and one in my money clip. Every time I go to pay for something, I see these values and am reminded of what's truly important to me. It's a big part of my personal game plan. I just have to ask in my best Samuel Jackson voice, "What's in *your* wallet?" Seriously, get your game plan in writing and keep it in a place where you'll see it regularly.

I need little reminders like that card because I'm not perfect. Far from it. I don't have the perfect marriage or perfect kids (but we do have the most perfect grandchildren, and I've got the pictures to prove it). It's important to remember that this journey we're on is a work in progress, and the most important thing is that you're working on it. That's what counts; that's what will get you closer to your destination.

The next two components to my plan have to do with family, so here's a little explanation about my value of "practice thriving family." I've learned that there are three types of families: dysfunctional, healthy, and thriving. To be perfectly honest, all of our families are dysfunctional in some ways; the lucky ones are functionally dysfunctional. For a long time I thought our goal should be to become a healthy family—one that's able to take care of itself. But I've changed my mind on that. It's great if your family takes care of itself, and God knows we need a lot more families who can do that. A thriving family, however, not only takes care of itself, but also takes care of other people and families. Imagine what our culture would look like if we had more thriving families.

Again, that's easy to say, but how do you include your family in your game plan? At an event I attended sponsored by my friends at the Halftime Institute, I was challenged by six questions that were aimed at helping us do just that:

* *Leadership.* What is your role in leading your family, and what is your vision for your family over the next thirty years? What do you need to do it well?

- *Values.* What are the core values that underpin your family as it grows? How will you help instill those values?
- *Family of unique individuals.* How well do you know your family members? What next level of understanding would most help you in your leadership role?
- *Serving.* Are there ways you can serve together as a family, and what is your role in that?
- *Legacy.* What legacy do you want to live out? How will you lead your family on a journey of generosity?
- *Celebrating.* How will you celebrate all of God's blessings in your family and what He's doing through you to bless others?

The one that really stuck out to me had to do with how well I knew my kids. As a businessman, I went out of my way to better understand my best clients—what they liked, what they didn't like, what they liked to eat or drink, and their favorite sports teams. I did this because it helped me serve them better, but when I went over that list of questions I just cited, I realized to my dismay that I knew more about my customers than I did about my kids. People who know me will read that and scratch their heads, but it's true. Yes, I have a good relationship with my kids, but did I really know them? Not as much as I should. So I included in my game plan what I call "family dreaming." I asked each of my kids to make a list of one hundred things they want to do between now and the time they leave this planet. After thirty or forty, they'll likely get stuck, but if you share them aloud together, you'll get to a hundred. I had them break it down into what they wanted to accomplish in the next twelve months, the next one to five years, and then five years and beyond. Their mother and I are sort of the co-CEOs of the family, and our goal is to help them find ways to realize their dreams.

After they made their lists, we sat down with each one and went over the list. It was an incredible experience! Talk about getting to know them better.

◆ ◆ ◆

What we have done as a society is take the really important things and trivialized them, and we've taken some trivial things and made them really important.
—Matthew Kelly

◆ ◆ ◆

But there are other ways, too. For example, I also gave them two books: *The Five Love Languages* by Gary Chapman and *Strengthsfinder 2.0* by Steven Rath. Both books help people understand themselves better, so I asked them to show me the results. Again, it helped me understand my kids so much better than I already did, but more importantly, it showed me how I can help them become the best they can be and show them that they are loved.

The important thing here is to take the time to really understand the unique person that each of your children is. If my ways don't appeal to you, come up with your own. Maybe it's as simple as setting aside some one-on-one time with each child. Ask the next question when you ask them how their day went. "So what does OK mean—what was the best part of your day? The worst?" Use a few vacation days to enjoy an overnighter with each child. Plan one "lifelong memory" per year with each child, which could be as simple as a father-daughter date night or spending a winter night with one of your kids, maybe even in a tent. You get the idea.

OUR FAMILY MISSION STATEMENT.

After attending a retreat, I began working on a family mission statement, which I then shared with our kids. To help you gain more clarity regarding where you are going as a family, I'm sharing it here and recommend you consider creating one for your own family.

The Sweeney Family Mission: to be a
healthy and thriving family

1. To be men and women for others
2. To help all our children, grandchildren, and spouses become the best version of themselves
3. To continuously help one another identify our passions and strengths and use them to serve others
4. To know and live that our family is rooted and united in God's love
5. To constantly be creating special MIT (moments in time) for one another, both small and big MIT
6. To leave a legacy of kindness, caring, and service to others
7. To create time and events together

One final note: if you're married or in a relationship, make your game plan a team project. The person you love often brings a fresh perspective to the process. He or she sometimes knows you better than you know yourself. This person can also be a helpful ally as you implement this plan individually and with your family.

As I was working on this chapter, Katie Ledecky had just swum to her fourth gold medal of the 2016 Rio Olympics. And she went out in style, setting a world record in her last event, the eight-hundred-meter freestyle. In an interview after that event, she was asked when in the race she thought she might set a world record, and she answered, "From the start. I knew that if I stayed with my plan I would swim fast." Her game plan was to go to Rio and win four gold medals. What's yours?

Go to the Tape

1. Describe what the ideal life would be for you and for your family.
2. List at least three things that you know you need to change in order to enjoy the life you always wanted.
3. How often do you set aside time to think seriously and strategically about the next twelve months, five to ten years, and ten years and beyond? Do you think that's sufficient?
4. Approximately 55 percent of American adults do not have a will or estate plan. Why do you think we are so reluctant to plan our lives?
5. If you have children, identify the following for each:
   a. Favorite movie
   b. Best friend's name
   c. Where he or she would like to go on the next vacation
   d. His or her least favorite class or subject in school and why
   e. At least one major ambition

CHAPTER 5

Move the Chains—What Gets Measured Gets Done

◆ ◆ ◆

TWO OLD JOCKS WHO HAVEN'T seen each other in years plan a reunion of sorts. They were teammates on their high school basketball team and decided it would be pretty cool, for old times' sake, to find a gym and go at it again, one-on-one. Probably not a good idea, since neither was in the best shape, but guys do things like that. In this case, no EMTs were needed—they made it through one game without serious injury, though it took forever to get to twenty-one points.

As they headed to the locker room to shower up, they dropped the basketball off at the equipment manager's window. The manager asked, "How'd it go?"

"Pretty good, actually!"

Pretty good is OK for those fifty-something warriors, but for today's *real* athletes, "pretty good" won't cut it. Ask them how they did after a game, and they'll rattle off a list of stats longer than your grocery list. That's because in professional sports, and even at the college level, everything gets measured. In the NFL, the stat guys measure solo tackles, tackles for loss, hurries, deflections, hits, knockdowns, sacks, attempted carries, yards gained, yards gained after a catch, field-goal percentage, and more. And then there's the quarterback, who's got a rating system that sounds like one big story problem: "Subtract thirty from the completion percentage, and multiply the result by 0.05. Then take the sum of the four categories, divide by six, and multiply by one hundred." Of course— makes perfect sense! But that resulting QBR can determine whether a quarterback gets a big payday, gets benched, or goes on waivers.

Major-league baseball is just as metrics crazy, as indicated by Michael Lewis in his book *Moneyball,* which addresses the importance of statistics in sports. Chicago Cubs pitcher Kyle Hendricks may not know how much he's contributed to his IRA, but you can be sure he knows his ERA (earned-run average, which was an amazing 2.19 when I wrote this chapter). Batters know their RBIs, SLG, PA/SO, TOB, GO/AO, and OBP, and if you know what those mean, I'm impressed.

If the NFL and other professional sports go crazy over stats, the business world makes them look like amateurs. Companies measure everything from the cost of goods sold to how many rolls of toilet paper they buy for their restrooms and everything in between. Apple may be a huge global company, but I'll bet the CFO knows exactly how many electronic devices they sold today, the manufacturing costs that went into each computer, and the expected profit from the sale of each device they sell.

Why so much emphasis on stats? Because according to business guru and author of *In Search of Excellence* Tom Peters, what gets measured gets done. Teams have their game plans, and businesses have their financial plans, but both are useless if you don't keep track of your progress toward those goals. Remember that big meeting before a football game in which the head coach goes over the game plan with his players? Well, there's another one after the game in which all the stats are handed out, and everyone can see how well—or how poorly—everyone else performed. Metrics in sports and business measure everything that contributes to the overall success of both.

If metrics are so important in sports and business, shouldn't they be important in our personal lives? Actually, they are. We measure a lot of things, but are they the right ones? We might measure the things we own. What happens when your neighbor pulls into his driveway in a new car? Not just any new car, but a BMW 6-Series. And you're driving a Ford, which is a great car, but it doesn't quite measure up to your neighbor's new ride. You just measured yourself based on a car. If it's not a car, it's a neighborhood. Yours is great, but three people in your neighborhood moved closer to the lake, to bigger homes with better views. "They must be doing a lot better than I am," you think. Page through magazines like *Vanity Fair* or *Fortune*. Those slick full-page ads you see are really metrics: measures of success. Meaning, you're not really successful until you own this watch or wear this brand. Maybe that's why I still read *Mad* magazine. Next to Alfred E. Neuman, I'm golden!

◆ ◆ ◆

How would you know if your life turned out really great, and what metrics would you use to measure whether it turned out well or not?

◆ ◆ ◆

Don't get me wrong. I like nice cars, and I think my home is a great place to create family memories. I'm not against having nice possessions, but after further review, it dawned on me—it's all just stuff. My value as a human being is not tied to any of it. The only thing a Rolex says about its owner is that he was willing to pay $10,000 for a watch. Period. He could be a great guy or a jerk. He could be living a life of meaning and purpose or careening from one personal crisis to another.

In his book *How Will You Measure Your Life?*, Clayton Christensen underscores the futility of measuring ourselves by the things we have:

> For many of us, one of the easiest mistakes to make is to focus on trying to oversatisfy the trappings of professional success in the mistaken belief that those things will make us happy. Better salaries. A more prestigious title. A nicer office. They are, after all, what our friends and family see as signs that we have "made it" professionally. But as soon as you find yourself focusing on the tangible aspects of your job, you are at risk of becoming like some of my classmates, chasing a mirage. The next pay raise, you think, will be the one that finally makes you happy. It's a hopeless quest.

◆ ◆ ◆

Think about the metric by which your life will be judged, and make a resolution to live every day so that in the end, your life will be judged a success.
—Clayton Christensen

◆ ◆ ◆

I also love the way Wayne Dyer speaks to this need of ours to own all the right things. He says, "I have a suit in my closet where the pockets are cut out. It's a reminder that I won't be taking anything with me." Or to put it another way, have you ever seen a U-Haul behind a hearse? Jesus warned against "earthly treasures" that rust or get eaten by moths. Rather, we may want to consider filling our lives with experiences because memories last forever.

We also measure our lives in terms of perceived status. You know, the PhD who insists on everyone calling her "Dr. So-and-so" or the guy who has to remind everyone he's the CEO. It happens at all levels. We measure ourselves with titles, awards that we hang on our walls, and being a little higher up on the org chart than some other guy. In other words, we focus on our "résumé values" (things we did in life) when we really need to pay more attention to our "eulogy values" (who we are as people and what we want to be remembered for). We all do it, or at least I have. And there's nothing wrong with promotions and titles, but you can have all the status that everyone else covets and still live a miserable life. We should be loving people and using things, but we've reversed it by loving things and using people.

I have a feeling that if you were on your deathbed, you wouldn't look back on your life and think, "Gee, I wish I would have bought more," or "Why didn't I make VP?" So how *should* we measure our lives? How would you know if your life turned out really great, and what metrics would you use to measure whether it turned out well or not? I got a lot of help on this from my personal coach, Lloyd Reeb, who wrote the book *From Success to Significance*. He guided me through some questions that appealed to me as a businessman. They may not be the final set of questions you use, but they should give you an idea of what might be the metrics of your personal life:

Asset protection. In business, it's vitally important that we protect our assets. Lose your assets, and you no longer have a business. In life, protecting what's most important to you is even more pivotal to enjoying meaning and purpose.

* What do you consider priceless in your life? Irreplaceable?
* What are you doing to protect it?

Cost accounting. When you run a business, you pay close attention to how much cost goes into a project or product. You may not realize it, but there are costs involved in how you live and work, which is likely how we got the phrase, "that took its toll on me."

* What is all your "success" costing you?
* As you make gains in your career and professional life, what are you losing in your personal life?

I can't tell you how many people I know who have accomplished great things in their careers but have left behind damaged relationships or fractured health. I believe it was the Dalai Lama who once said, "People lose their health to make money, only to spend their money to regain their health." Your metrics for the game of life need to measure the costs associated with the way you have chosen to live, and once you tally it up, answer this question as honestly as you can: Is it worth it? And if it isn't, what steps must you take to reduce those costs?

Metrics. If your life turned out great, what would it look like? What are the specifics that you could measure to determine how well you are doing? My friend and mentor, Bob Buford, inherited a reasonably successful business and with a lot of hard work turned it into a *really* successful business—so much so that at a fairly young age he could retire and spend the rest of his life playing golf or going on cruises. Instead, he began a period of reflection, thinking about his mission in life and how he would accomplish it. He felt he was put on this earth for a higher purpose than making money or coasting through the second half of his life. As a Christian, he had a passion to see large churches become more effective and began funding various initiatives toward that goal. His mission was to transform the latent energy in American Christianity into active energy. In other words, he wanted to get religious people off their butts and encourage them to do the hard things Jesus taught them to do that would make the world a better place. Bob has given away a lot of money to make that happen, and one of his metrics is the growth of what's become called the megachurch—churches with more than two thousand active adherents. When he started in 1985, there were fewer than five hundred megachurches in the United States. Today there are 1,650, and most can point to Bob's influence. In fact, he may be the most influential Christian you've never heard of until now. His own mentor, the late Peter Drucker, said of him, "His fruit grows on other people's trees."

One of the first things I did was develop my personal mission statement: "To use my energy, enthusiasm, and network to inspire others to do positive things they never thought they could do." I intentionally chose the word "inspire" instead of "motivate" because motivation is like cotton candy—it's colorful and fun and makes you feel good for a few hours, but then it disappears in your mouth. You go back to your same old habits; nothing has changed. Besides, motivation is usually all about getting people to do what they don't want to do. I want to inspire people to do something really positive and great.

But how can I measure that? How will I know if I'm making any progress? I decided to give myself a metric: between now and when I leave this earth, I will inspire a million people. Gulp! That's a lot. Or at least, that's what I thought at the time. But then I thought about one of the songs I was learning to play on my guitar, "I'm Yours" by Jason Mraz. I googled the song and discovered it had garnered more than 247 million views. It dawned on me that in this age of social media, a million isn't all that great. I adjusted my goal and now am committed to inspiring *one hundred million* people to do things in a positive way that they never thought they could do. It sounds impossible, but what if I inspired only a hundred people, who in turn each inspired a million? Mission accomplished. And imagine what could happen if those one hundred million people in turn inspired another million each? My calculator won't even go that high!

Bob also inspired me to identify my "perfect life values." To make sure I lived out those values, I had them printed on a card, which I laminated and keep in my wallet so that every time I open my wallet, I see that card and ask myself, "What specifically have you done to live out these values?" It's important that you focus on specifics rather than generalities. For example, if you've set a health goal to lose weight, how much weight? What specific weight do you want to get to? If you can't measure it, you probably won't lose much weight at all.

When I share with others my personal mission of influencing one hundred million people, they usually say things like, "Why is it so important to put a number to your goal? Can't you just say you want to inspire a lot of people?" It gets back to those old ex-jocks after their impromptu game of one-on-one. Who wants to say at the end of their life, "I did a pretty good job"? Remember, what gets measured gets done. Measuring your progress ensures that you will indeed make progress. The data that your metrics provide will help you get clearer, help you continually reenergize, and inspire you to get better every day—not better than others, but better than what you were yesterday. I need to remind myself of that because I'm pretty competitive. I'm a broken-down old jock, which means that with each year of looking back at my playing days, I'm better than I really was. In fact, the older I get, the better I was!

I used to work hard to be better than anyone else, but after further review, I quit measuring myself against others and now worry only about becoming a better me.

In the previous chapter, I invited you to create a game plan for your life. If you really want to live out that game plan, you need to be able to measure it. For example, if one of your goals was to enjoy better health, consider these examples of metrics for your physical lifestyle:

* I will give myself thirty to forty-five minutes of aerobic exercise at least five days a week.
* I will avoid foods that have been determined to contribute to heart disease and increase my intake of foods that have been found to improve heart health.
* I will quit smoking.
* I will get a complete physical exam at least once a year.

By holding yourself accountable to specific, measurable actions like these, you will have a much greater chance of actually enjoying growing older. Remember, what gets measured gets done.

◆ ◆ ◆

**The journey of a thousand miles
begins with a single step.
—Lao Tzu**

◆ ◆ ◆

Will I make it to one hundred million? Maybe. Maybe not. So why is this so critically important? Because it helps us organize our days, weeks, and years—hopefully the rest of our lives. It helps us decide what to do every day when we get up in the morning, and it also helps us make decisions about who we want to spend time with, what we want to do, and how we're going to do it. When you have metrics for your life, it helps you stay focused on your mission so that when you approach the end, you'll be able to enjoy the satisfaction that comes from a life lived well. Instead of pointing to a garage full of toys, a sizeable net worth, or accolades from your colleagues at work, you'll page through a life filled with the snapshots of those whom you have influenced for the better. I actually do that—literally. A friend gave me the idea to create a "book of days," where I collect thoughts and artifacts from everyday life to celebrate all the good that I experience, as opposed to the things that I own.

Harvard professor Clayton Christensen reminds us what really counts in life:

> You know those cartoons where some poor guy is standing in front of the pearly gates and Saint Peter is there with a big ledger book? If we are indeed asked to give an account of ourselves when our lives end, I don't think we're going to get very far if we start listing the awards we've been given, the promotions that came our way, or the wealth we've amassed. Instead, I believe we're going to be asked questions like, "What have you done for others?" "Who is a better person because of you?" "On how many people can I find your fingerprints of kindness, encouragement, and compassion?" These are the metrics each of us needs to be compiling, one day at a time…God, in contrast to us, does not need the tools of statisticians or accountants. So far as I know, he has no organization charts. There is no need to aggregate anything beyond the level of an individual person in order to comprehend completely what is going on among humankind. His only measure of achievement is the individual.

This brings us back to the gridiron. One of the cool things about football is that at any given moment, you can visually see how a team is making progress toward its goal of getting into the end zone. I'm talking about the yard marker and the chains that measure the ten yards needed for a first down. If a kick returner gets nailed on the one-yard line, then when the offense comes out on the field, they're looking at a long ninety-nine yards to pay dirt. It's pretty overwhelming, except they don't have to do it all at once. Just get ten yards over the next three plays, and you "move the chains." Keep doing it, and you'll eventually put six points up on the board.

Likewise, you don't have to reach your life's metrics overnight. You just need to keep moving the chains. Or, as Lao Tzu says, "The journey of a thousand miles begins with a single step." Life may tackle you occasionally when it's third and long, but you get another chance. And another. And another. And soon that goal line will be right in front of you, and you'll be able to look back down the field and see just how far you've come. Whether you actually get into the end zone—whether I ever reach one hundred million—is not as important as the fact that by giving yourself a measurable goal, you will accomplish more than you can imagine.

Especially if you have enough of the right kind of energy.

Go to the Tape

1. What are the metrics of your professional life? How are you measured at work?
2. Look at each of the following, and rank on a scale of one (low) to ten (high) where you are today. Then determine where you need to focus more attention. What do you need to do to make the lower ones higher?

a. Work and career
b. Marriage and family
c. Income and money
d. Health
e. Awards and recognition
f. Relationships and friends
g. Possessions and toys
h. Spirituality
i. Service to others

3. Go back over the list above, and try to assess what percentage of your time and effort goes into each.
4. Pick three of the above categories that are important to you, and identify at least one measurable goal for each.

CHAPTER 6
Energy—the Hidden Differential On and Off the Field

◆ ◆ ◆

Everything is energy and that's all there is to it.
Match the frequency of the reality you want and
you cannot help but get that reality. It can be no
other way. This is not philosophy. This is physics.

—ALBERT EINSTEIN

THROUGHOUT MY CAREER IN SPORTS and business, I've had the opportunity to observe up close and personal a lot of high-level performers: athletes, CEOs, and top salespeople. Recently, I was given the privilege of watching some of the toughest, smartest, competitive guys on the planet: the navy SEALs. Over the past few years I got to spend several days with them as they endured the sheer torture of physical and psychological challenges. But even before they become SEALs, they have to get through "hell week"—five and a half days of brutally difficult training on less than four hours of sleep.

I've also seen my share of average and below-average performers in sports and business (never from a SEAL—you can't be a slacker and a SEAL). You've probably seen them, too: a wide receiver who won't run his route at 100 percent if he knows the pass is going to someone else, a defensive lineman who runs out of steam in the fourth quarter, and the guy in the cubicle next to you who shuts down around three in the afternoon.

Based on my informal research and experience, I can tell you that one of the biggest differences between high-level performers and the rest of us is energy. It's the secret sauce that turns average performances into spectacular displays of strength and endurance.

It's that kind of energy that Garth Brooks displayed when he came to Milwaukee. He initially booked the Bradley Center for a Friday night concert, but the eighteen-thousand-seat arena sold out in less than an hour. When Steve Costello, president of the Bradley Center, passed that information on to Brooks, the superstar offered to play a Saturday show to accommodate such incredible fan interest. Once announced, that one also sold out in ten minutes. So what did Brooks do? Added a *second* concert on Saturday, meaning he would perform an unheard of three shows in twenty-seven hours. All this as he was in the middle of a demanding tour schedule.

I attended the first two shows and was absolutely floored. I've been to a few concerts featuring top artists, and you're lucky if they stay on stage for an hour to an hour and a half. Brooks played for two and a half hours, nonstop! But he didn't just strum his guitar and sing. The guy was all over the stage, connecting with the audience with his charismatic personality that never wavered during the entire two-and-a-half-hour set. Then he did it twice on Saturday. Talk about energy.

Have you ever met someone who just seemed to exude energy? And what about you? Do you ever find yourself running out of gas—physically or emotionally—miles before the next gas station?

◆ ◆ ◆

One of the biggest differences between high-level performers and the rest of us is energy. It's the secret sauce that turns average performances into spectacular displays of strength and endurance.

◆ ◆ ◆

If you're in your twenties, you can probably skip this chapter because you likely have energy to burn. It's just the way we roll when we're young, which is why most of us could eat as much as we wanted of everything and never gain a pound. But as we burn through our thirties, life has a way of catching up with us. Now when you see that mountain, you don't have a burning desire to climb it for the same reason you used to charge right up: it's there. Work, family, and other obligations—along with changes in metabolism—settle onto our shoulders like the sixty-pound backpacks the SEALs carry with ease. Only for us, it feels like a sixty-pound backpack. You begin to accept a little slower pace because, well, it's inevitable—until you see someone in her sixties running circles around you.

Energy makes the difference between performing well in all aspects of life and doing your best to be just a little better than average. It's what helps you contribute in that 3:00 p.m. meeting on Friday instead of fighting to stay awake. One of the things I love about energy is that it's contagious. Just hanging out with energetic people can increase your own energy levels. But energy doesn't just happen. It's not something you're born with; it's a force you tap into. How? To understand that, we need to take a closer look at three types of energy available to all of us: physical, emotional, and spiritual. While we'll look at each separately, they really overlap. For example, a good workout gives me a boost in my physical energy, but maybe more importantly, I feel more alive emotionally and spiritually when I work out regularly. The goal here is to reflect on how the way you live can connect you with greater sources of energy.

Physical Energy

Regaining or increasing your physical energy is simple but not easy. Simple, because physical energy is built on three foundations: food, sleep, and movement. In other words, if you want greater energy, eat right, rest properly, and work out regularly. Actually *doing* those three things is another story, which is why more than one-third of American adults are obese and another third overweight. (Disclaimer: This isn't a diet or fitness book, but it's tough to be out of shape and have a high energy level. If you need proof, try this experiment. Put four five-pound bags of sugar into an empty backpack, put the backpack on, and walk around for a few minutes. Feel energetic? Probably not.)

Food as Fuel

Two entirely different technological inventions have radically changed our health and energy levels. The first is actually a series of new farming methods and technology, which has improved agricultural production and in turn greatly increased the availability of many different kinds of foods. Two in particular have contributed to our increase in weight and subsequent decrease in energy. According to a number of sources, back in the 1700s, the average American ate five pounds of sugar and five pounds of wheat per year. Today we eat an average of 150 pounds of sugar and 133 pounds of wheat. So for starters, get rid of as much sugar and wheat in your diet as possible. Replace it with all those things you know are good for you: fresh fruits, vegetables, nuts, and so on.

Think of food as fuel, not a treat or reward for all your hard work. If you travel for business, that won't be easy: after a long day on the job, eating on an expense account appears to be a well-earned perk. Except those road meals are packed with fat, salt, and carbohydrates—the triple play that kills energy and increases weight gain. Also, try to avoid processed foods, which rely heavily on those deadly three but throw in a staggering list of chemicals and other additives that you don't need and have questionable health value.

Again, I'm no nutritionist, but here are a few quick tips on how to eat for energy:

* *Avoid second helpings.* Many of us usually still feel hungry after finishing a meal. Wait about ten minutes, and that feeling will go away.
* *Don't clean up your plate when eating out.* Restaurant helpings are huge, and we feel we need to eat it all to get our money's worth. Ask for a box, and eat the rest for lunch the next day. Being a member of the clean-plate club is way overrated.
* *Drink water.* Dehydration has been linked to depression, lethargy, and headaches. Bare minimum: eight ounces, eight times a day, or roughly eight glasses of water per day.

In addition to the health benefits, drinking water gives you a "full" feeling, so you eat less.

* *Incorporate healthy snacks.* An apple or a handful of nuts is better than sneaking a candy bar.
* *Avoid fast food.* Big Macs, Whoppers, fries, soda, and milkshakes are not high-energy foods. They're not even that fast anymore.

POWERED BY SLEEP

The second major technological invention affecting our energy levels is actually another form of energy: electricity. Before electricity was made widely available in our homes, the average American slept between ten and twelve hours a night. Once artificial lighting became the norm, the amount of sleep decreased to a little over six and a half hours per night. It's almost become a badge of honor for some of us: "Yeah, I only need three hours of sleep, and I'm ready to go." My response is, "For how long?" Studies have shown that for as little as a half hour of missed sleep, you will be less alert the next day. This makes me think that getting an extra half an hour of sleep will likely contribute to greater energy. Here are some ways to ensure you're getting enough sleep:

* *Go to bed earlier.* Duh! But in addition to getting back that half hour of sleep, you'll be healthier, as studies have shown that staying up late causes a variety of harms to the body.[1]
* *Keep a consistent sleep schedule.* A study of mice in 2013 found that varying their sleep schedules increased inflammatory diseases. Next time you see a mouse, thank him for participating in the study, and stick to a regular bedtime.

---

1 http://www.lookchem.com/Chempedia/Health-and-Chemical/2924.html.

- *Don't eat within an hour of going to bed.* Lying down after eating can contribute to heartburn and indigestion.
- *Avoid alcohol and caffeine in the evening.* A glass of wine might make you feel drowsy and thus help you get to sleep quicker, but the alcohol often disrupts your sleeping later in the night.
- *Don't exercise before going to bed.* As you're about to learn, exercise gives you an energy jolt, so you'll have a hard time falling to sleep.
- *Turn off electronic devices one hour before you go to bed.* All the research shows that light stimulates the brain.

BURN ENERGY TO GAIN ENERGY

Your great-grandparents probably worked out eight hours a day or more: walking behind a plow horse, splitting wood, and throwing bales of hay into the hayloft. And—of course—walking seven miles to school. Barefoot. In a snowstorm. Today, most of what we do for a living is sedentary. We drive to work, ride an elevator to the fifteenth floor, sit in front of a computer, and maybe walk to the candy machine a couple of times a day. Then we go back down the elevator, drive home, eat supper, and slide into the La-Z-Boy to watch TV for a couple of hours.

And you wonder how you put on a "few" extra pounds and run out of steam early in the day?

Regular exercise will not only shed some of that weight, but it actually increases your energy levels. In the short run, you get a huge rush of energy after working out. In the long run, your cardiovascular system—heart and lungs—will reward you with greater endurance. And your exercise doesn't have to be a gut-busting workout that leaves you gasping for air. Most exercise physiologists consider walking the perfect exercise. Thirty minutes a day of walking will strengthen your heart health; forty-five minutes will contribute to weight loss. Either of those regimens alone will improve your energy levels.

Emotional Energy

In addition to gaining energy by taking better care of your body, you stand to gain or lose energy by the way you choose to live. For example, I'm a gym rat—even before I start working out, I get energized just by hanging out at health clubs. I also gain energy from the soothing, peaceful atmosphere in a church or my home library. For you, it may be walking along a beach or sitting quietly in a park or forest. Take a moment to reflect on the places where you find yourself energized just by being there. If you want more energy in your life, make it a point to visit those places regularly.

The same thing is true about the activities we engage in and even the people we hang out with. A few years ago, I decided to teach myself fifty songs on the guitar, and as I began practicing I discovered that I was energized by those sessions. Ditto when I read a good book or attend a sporting event. I try to program more of these activities into my life, avoiding activities that tend to drain my energy levels (like standing in line at the DMV). Here again, reflect on the activities that tend to leave you feeling energized. Do you have a hobby that you need to spend more time enjoying? Maybe it's attending a classical music concert or walking through an art museum. Too often we let the busyness of life squeeze those energizing activities out and then wonder why we feel as if we're stuck in a rut.

Now here's the tough one. One of the most important factors that can raise or lower your energy levels is people—who you're spending the majority of your time with, who you're surrounding yourself with. I'm not the first person who's said this, but "we're all the average of the five people we spend the most time with." Who are you hanging out with more than anyone else? Who are those five people both professionally and personally, and are they people who give you energy or deplete your energy? When I ask people to make a list of those people, it scares them because in most cases they discover two or three out of the five are energy drainers, and they need to disconnect from them. That's hard, but what's more important to you? Hanging on to a relationship that leaves you exhausted or living at your maximum potential? Make your list, and if you're uncomfortable ditching those two or three people dragging you down, at least find ways to spend a little less time with them.

◆ ◆ ◆

Energy makes the difference between performing well in all aspects of life and doing your best to be just a little better than average.

◆ ◆ ◆

SPIRITUAL ENERGY

Three things you can't talk about without getting yourself into trouble: politics, sex, and religion. I'm about to get into trouble because I'm going to venture into the sacred world of the, well, sacred. And I do this recognizing that you may be Christian, Jewish, Muslim, Buddhist, New Age, agnostic, atheist (currently called "nones" among younger people), or a combination of the above.

I'll begin with a disclaimer: I am a Catholic – maybe best defined as an evangelical Catholic. Born and raised in the faith, I rarely miss showing up for Mass. However, like some American Catholics, I was raised and catechized during a time of change and confusion in the sixties. Having said that, I believe all knowledge comes from God. Along with scripture, I have studied ancient and current wisdom from many different sources. I believe we can learn from so many of the great thinkers, from Aristotle to the Founding Fathers. It's just that sometimes the way they talk about the unseen or spiritual world makes sense to me, fills in some of the gaps in my own catechesis, and actually makes me a better Catholic.

Regardless of your own personal beliefs, I am convinced that there is a spiritual or divine energy that is always present. It's the "high" you get from working out or sitting in a cathedral, finishing a long run, or hanging out with a great friend. For me, that energy is God, or some may call it divine energy, a higher power, or life force. It's not so important what you call it; it's important that you experience it, which I believe we all have, if even briefly. For example, even if you're not a religious person, when you witness a breathtaking sunrise in the mountains, hear your newborn cry for the first time, or find yourself engrossed in a powerful novel, you likely feel as if time and space have stopped momentarily and that you have been transported to another level or plane. That's what I define as tapping into spiritual energy, and our goal is to figure out how to get connected to this energy and stay connected for longer periods of time. Not to get all spooky with you, but the only time we will experience it without interruption is when we die. In the meantime, we do our best to fill our lives with those things that give us this kind of connection to the almighty.

That's why I carry a little twig in my pocket. During my ongoing conversations with Sister Camille, a ninety-four-year-old nun, she taught me the importance of staying "connected to the vine." She was referring to Jesus, who in the Gospel of John said, "I am the vine; you are the branches. If you remain in me and I in you, you will bear much fruit..." I keep that twig in my pocket to represent the vine, and every time I reach into my pocket and feel it there, it reminds me to stay connected.

How many times a day do you reach for food or a snack? If you're like most people, you eat three meals a day and probably grab a snack a couple of other times. Let's say we eat five times a day. Does it make any sense that many churches offer one service a week to connect to God? Sister Camille prays five times a day, so maybe that's a good place to start—five times a day, do something deliberate that connects you with a higher power. It could be a brief prayer, a few minutes of meditation, or reading a brief passage from a sacred text of the religion you practice. In addition to the twig I carry, I also set my cell phone alarm to beep every hour to remind me to stop and say a brief prayer. You might pause at your desk a few times during the day, close your eyes, and simply think or meditate about God. The important thing is to take care of yourself spiritually as much as you do physically.

What I find so cool about the way all of this energy interacts is that this God-force working through us becomes a magnet. As Catholics, we are taught that by allowing the Holy Spirit to work through us, we live out our faith in ways that draw people to us. Jesus said that the two greatest commandments are to love God and love our neighbors. On our own, that's difficult, but by tapping into the energy of the Holy Spirit—or if you prefer, divine energy—we reflect that energy in ways that attract others. Or as Saint Paul wrote, we embody the very qualities or "fruit" of the Holy Spirit: love, joy, peace, forbearance, kindness, goodness, faithfulness, gentleness, and self-control (Gal. 5:22–23).

There's an added benefit to tapping into the spiritual or divine. According to Dan Buettner, author of *Blue Zones,* numerous studies find that in general, religious or spiritual people tend to be happier than nonreligious people, tend to participate less in risky behaviors, and even live longer than people with no connection to a faith community.

As I said, I'm not trying to convert you. But I would love for you to at least consider ways to tap into this type of energy. If you were raised in a faith tradition and have drifted away, give it another shot. You were probably younger, someone said or did something to you that you didn't like, or you just weren't dialed in that much. Dig a little deeper in the core beliefs of your faith community. Immerse yourself in its sacred texts. Seek out someone you respect from that tradition, and begin a conversation. You may see things differently than you once did and experience more frequently its benefits.

If you've never been religious, set aside any assumptions you have about religion or religious people, and focus on being open to ideas that live in the spiritual realm. Go and visit a house of worship. As I said earlier, you don't have to be religious to experience the spiritual energy that I believe is always present. However, you may find that your views on religion have been formed more by the "bad examples" present in all religions and not on the actual teachings of religious communities. Or, to put it another way, "Do unto others as you would have them do unto you," is a pretty good rule to live by, and it happens to be a distinctly religious teaching that is found in the New Testament as well as in the sacred texts of many religions.

Our relationships with God are in actuality so much more than mere tools for us to succeed or benefits of added energy that we receive here on earth. As the Desiderata, attributed to Max Ehrmann, states, "Therefore be at peace with God, whatever you conceive Him to be, and whatever your labors and aspirations, in the noisy confusion of life keep peace with your soul." Knowing this alone is energizing.

FUEL FOR LIFE'S JOURNEY

As we spend more time taking care of our bodies, engaging in positive activities with positive people, and connecting more regularly to spiritual resources, we will become naturally drawn to those things. In other words, we won't have to work so hard to experience them—they will come naturally.

Albert Einstein was right: everything is energy. Give your body the right fuel. Engage in some type of regular, sustained exercise. Get enough rest. Program activities, places, and people in your life that deliver energy (and avoid those that deplete energy). And stay connected to the Vine—a higher power or universal energy. All of these sources of energy I've covered here are really just different ways to connect to the energy that I call God. Call it whatever you want, but when you tap into it, your life will become connected with something higher, greater than you, enabling you to live not just for the moment, but forever.

Go to the Tape

1. On a scale of one to ten, with ten being "off-the-charts energetic," rate your current energy level.
2. In what ways do you think unhealthy habits are related to your energy level?
3. Approximately how much time do you spend each day doing some type of physical exercise or activity?
4. Identify at least one source of energy for the following categories:
    a. Activity (e.g., reading, listening to music, pursuing a hobby)
    b. Place (e.g., house of worship, art gallery, coffee shop)
    c. Person (one from your work and one from your personal life)
5. Using the same list above, identify one source that tends to be energy draining for you.
6. Describe an experience or moment when you felt a sense of awe or marvel. What could you do to experience that feeling more frequently? What can you do to connect each day and tap into some spiritual energy?
7. Program your phone or timer every hour to pause and pray, reflect, and give thanks.

CHAPTER 7

The Four Quarters of Life

◆ ◆ ◆

For everything there is a season, and a time
for every purpose under heaven.

—Ecclesiastes 3:1

Let's assume you're in your forties or fifties. Do you ever wonder what it's like for a twelve-year-old just entering middle school? I mean, 9/11 is ancient history to them—they weren't even alive then. And what are they going to be like when they graduate from college, get "downsized" from a great job, visit their parents in a retirement center, and begin taking Social Security?

I think a lot about concepts like this.

For some reason, I've always been intrigued by the various stages of human life. Even as a teenager, I wondered what life looked like to a twelve-year-old versus what it looked like to a seventy-year-old or even a ninety-year-old. Maybe I fixated on this topic because I grew up in a large family with literally hundreds of cousins, aunts, and uncles representing multiple generations. What was Grandpa Murphy thinking when he was sitting on the front porch smoking his hand-rolled cigarettes? As a boy, he lived before the automobile had been invented and in his lifetime witnessed not only the dawn of the car but also the beginnings of airplanes, jets, rockets, and even a man walking on the moon. As the ninth of ten kids, I'd wonder what it must have been like for my older brothers to leave home for college, get married, and start families.

In college, I researched and read several books on the way we make our way through the various stages of life. Even though it was thirty-five years ago, I can still recall the two books that focused my interest on this topic from a more academic perspective: *The Seasons of a Man's Life* by Daniel Levinson and *Passages* by Gail Sheehy. I devoured these books, which led me to write my final paper on the topic for my developmental psychology class. I'm pretty sure I got an A, but what I recall most is how learning about the seasons of life was one of the most transformational changes in my own life. How? It helped me understand the seemingly simple quote at the beginning of this chapter—"For everything there is a season, and a time for every purpose under heaven."

◆ ◆ ◆

You can have it all, just not all at once.

◆ ◆ ◆

We see that in sports. With the exception of the sprints in racing sports like swimming or track and field, you can't go all out for the entire contest. In those aforementioned sports, there's a pacing that goes on that allows you to finish strong. In a distance race, for example, a runner might start fast, then ease into a comfortable pace, reserving enough energy for the final "kick" down the straightaway. In team sports like basketball and football, that pacing is often determined by the way the game is divided into halves and quarters. In professional basketball and football, each of the four quarters has a distinctive quality or character based on the recognition that you can't play all four quarters the same way. What these sports have in common is a break in the middle of the game to regroup and make adjustments in order to go back out on the field and win.

In life, we have the same opportunities. My friend and mentor Bob Buford used the concept of "halftime" to describe how to make the necessary adjustments in life so that you can make the transition from success to significance. I've been so influenced by his book, appropriately titled *Halftime*, that I've bought hundreds for my friends and acquaintances over the years. Bob's take on halftime as a successful businessman mirrors what Carl Jung, one of my all-time favorite authors, wrote about the first and second halves of life. Jung saw the first forty or so years of life as a time when we establish identities—going to school, starting careers, and entering into and developing relationships. Then in the second half of life, we begin to focus more on finding and nurturing our souls and developing a deeper sense of purpose. Jung referred to these two seasons as the "morning" and "afternoon" of life.

◆ ◆ ◆

At the stroke of noon, the descent [of the sun] begins,
and the descent means the reversal of all ideals
and values that were cherished in the morning.
—Carl Jung

◆ ◆ ◆

He went on to explain that you can't live the second half of life with the same rules that you followed in the first half.

Except most of us think we can, and that's why so many people miss out on the incredible adventure that awaits them into their fifties, sixties, seventies, and beyond. That's why reflection is so critical to our ability to thrive rather than just hang on and survive. After further review, you'll see more clearly how the game of life is changing as well as what you must do to adapt to those changes in a way that makes each stage of life better than the previous one.

As much as I appreciate the way both Buford and Jung divide life into two segments, I've come to look at life as the four quarters of a football game. Maybe it's the result of being a sports junkie, but here's the way I describe the stages of life that we all must negotiate.

First Quarter

One of the most exciting moments in a football game is when the teams charge out of the tunnel and onto the field before lining up for the opening kickoff. It doesn't matter what the odds are; both teams are confident they'll win. They can't wait to get out there and establish their dominance. And that's a pretty good description of the first quarter of life. It's the first twenty-five to thirty-five or so years that include getting an education and a good job and possibly starting a family. It's a period when our unbridled eagerness and healthy optimism convince us that we can do anything, be anything. And driving us during this stage of life is an incredible energy, partly because we're so young, but also from the very newness of our life's experiences: finding and falling in love with the right person, buying your first house, welcoming children into your life, or promotions at work. Of course, you suffer setbacks—we all do—but in this first quarter we're resilient. We bounce back. It's like the University of Texas Longhorns getting embarrassed by Notre Dame 38–3 one year, then coming back the next year and all but taking the fight out of the Irish in an exciting upset.

What the first quarter of life is all about is establishing your identity. It's going from being your parents' son or daughter to becoming your own person. Maybe the best way to describe arriving at the end of the first quarter of life is through a commercial that was popular a few years ago. Two men are enjoying a meal in restaurant, obviously a father who appears to be in his early fifties, and his son, a young man approaching thirty. When the server delivers the check at the end of the meal, both reach for it as a voiceover says, "Is it that time?" The son picks up the check.

The end of the first quarter is "that time" when you know who you are and take the responsibility that comes with that knowledge.

SECOND QUARTER

For most people, the second quarter of life is all about hanging on and keeping up. By hanging on, I mean when you're in your thirties and forties, you're experiencing some of the busiest and potentially draining years you'll ever live. You're trying your best to balance work-life issues, with both demanding from you more than you can possibly give. Your kids are at the stage where they're involved in school, sports, band, youth groups, and sleepovers. You live under the constant fear that it's your turn to pick them up after school, but you're stuck in a meeting at work that's running long. You're proud of each promotion you've been given but quickly learn that the higher you climb, the more responsibility falls on your shoulders.

Then there's the keeping up. In the second quarter, we tend to measure our value by the possessions we have—or, more accurately, the things we don't have but that our neighbors do. Naturally, when your neighbor or a colleague at work drives in with a new car, you start shopping for one. But once you get it, you're stressed out over the fact that your car payments are a lot higher than they were on the car you just traded in. After further review, we begin to wonder why we buy things we don't need with money we don't have to impress people we don't like.

Great questions.

It's in the second quarter that we're most vulnerable to the myth that we can have it all. We've both seen it happen, right? Like the rapidly rising CPA at the prestigious accounting firm—when I first met her, she had four kids under ten years old. Her star kept rising; full partner was easily in her future. In many ways, she had the ideal life, except that she was frazzled all the time, always in a hurry, and never seemed to really enjoy life. I believe the main reason for her chronic discomfort with her life was that she was trying to have it all. Right now. That's the challenge of the second quarter. It's like the favored team having to play catch-up football throughout the first two quarters of the game.

The busyness of the second quarter likely won't change, but you can change the way you handle it. Taking time to reflect may be more important during this season in life than in any other. With so much going on, your priorities can become blurred as you try to do it all and have it all. Are all those things delivering what you thought they would? If not, are you willing to make the changes that will give you your life back? And if you are, how do you do it? You head for the locker room.

THE HALFTIME LOCKER ROOM

What does every football team do after the second quarter? It heads to the locker room to hit the pause button, reflect on what did or didn't work during the first two quarters, and then make the necessary adjustments. We can do the same thing.

A few years ago, my brother Mike, a businessman, headed for the locker room. Once he got inside and reflected on how he had been playing the game, he realized he didn't want to be a businessman, so he made a really big adjustment. Despite being a husband and father to a wife and four kids, he got his PhD in counseling, completely changing his career. It wasn't easy, but he knew that was what he had to do to be able to enjoy the rest of the game.

Not everyone who goes into the locker room will decide they have to change careers. Some decide they like the way the game is going and tweak it a bit by volunteering for a nonprofit or deliberately carving out more meaningful time with their families. Your main goal in the locker room is to determine if you're investing your time and talent in things that truly matter to you, and if not, determine what needs to change so that you are.

THIRD QUARTER

The third quarter—roughly the late forties and into the sixties—has the potential to be the most dynamic, productive stage of your life. It can also be a period of gradual decline: putting your life on autopilot and going through the motions rather than grabbing life by the horns. Many describe this stage as getting stuck in a rut—the best definition of a rut I've ever heard is "a grave with the ends knocked out."

It's in the third quarter that what I referred to earlier as a "smoldering discontent" begins to appear. The things that energized you in the second quarter no longer create the same excitement or satisfaction that they once did. You have this sense that there must be more to life than closing deals or attending meetings, but you don't quite know what it is. How you play the game in the third quarter of your life will be determined by how you respond to the amazing reality that you have at least another thirty years of horsepower and skills under the hood.

Some decide to slow down when they run out on the field in the third quarter. In football, that's called "playing not to lose," involving conservative, safe play calling, trying to hold on until the end of the game. In the game of life, it's settling in, not trying anything new, and avoiding risk. Or for some who can afford it, it means cashing in and living the life of leisure, doing pretty much whatever you please. Neither option delivers the kind of dynamic, meaningful lives we truly desire. I believe that's because we're all created for a purpose. I've got a better option for your third quarter: make it the best season of your life thus far, and that will happen when you let your passions and your dreams determine how you will live. In other words, after further review of your life—your work, your family and other relationships, and the things you are most passionate about— what adjustments do you need to make in order to spend more time on the things that really matter? It's the third quarter I'm in right now, and I gotta tell you, I'm having a blast. And you can, too. Here's how.

First, take a look at what you bring to the table. By this time in your life, you have enormous capacity as well as fewer obligations such as younger children and the demands of a career. You have a wealth of experience and the concurrent wisdom that it brings. Unlike your ancestors, you likely didn't till the fields or stand all day at an assembly line, so you're in relatively good health. In other words, you have a lot going for you, so why not invest some of this capacity into the things that really excite you? I'm not talking about quitting your job and going to volunteer for your house of worship, but staying in the game and using your additional time and talents to make this world a better place. In the process, you'll discover the life you've always wanted.

For example, after further review in my third quarter, I learned that I really get high on generosity. The simple act of helping someone who's having a hard go of it does more for me than it does for them. If you have learned anything about me by now, you know I sort of go all in on things, so instead of keeping a few dollars in my pocket to give away, I stop at the bank every week and get a bunch of two-dollar bills. I just love the looks I get when, in addition to a tip I give to the wonderful lady who serves up lunch for me at the little snack shop in my building, I hand her a couple of two-dollar bills. I happen to know that she's a single mom working hard to provide for her children, and that extra money means an awful lot to her. Am I changing the world by doing this? Probably not. But every time I do this, at least two people end up feeling pretty great, and that's not a bad ROI. I also find myself going through my closets periodically and taking all those nice clothes I had to have to a shelter downtown. In addition to these smaller, serendipitous generosity events, I've stretched a bit and invested more significantly in the lives of others, something I might not have done if I had decided to just hang on in my third quarter.

The point is not, "Hey, look how generous I am." Instead, it's the result of reflecting on what's important to me and using my third quarter to program more of this into my life. You might have a passion for keeping younger teenagers out of trouble or helping newly arrived immigrants get established in your community. And what matters most to you doesn't have to be some altruistic endeavor. I've always wanted to be able to play the guitar, so in my third quarter I've resolved to learn how to play fifty songs. In your third quarter, you have more freedom to pursue those passions, so why would you ever miss out on this opportunity to live a more fulfilled, purposeful life?

Now here's a necessary dose of reality. The third quarter can be tougher than the first two. Statistics show a surge in divorce among those fifty and older. Even with our efforts to stay healthy, we have heart attacks. Cancer. Companies downsize and always seem to keep the thirty-somethings, leaving the fifty-three-year-old trying to find a job. Life just doesn't always turn out the way we thought it would, even after reviewing it more carefully in the locker room. When those things happen, however, we have a choice. You can embrace the challenge facing you and handle it on your terms, or you can let it determine your outlook and your attitude. I love the way Richard Rohr addresses this in his book *Falling Upward*. He says that we have a choice when we hit sharp points in life: we can fall down, or we can see this as an opportunity to grow and fall upward. Rohr states that wisdom is simply healed pain.

As I mentioned in the first chapter, last year was the best year of my life, but I'm halfway through this year, and it might even top last year. And I expect next year to go pretty well too. The same thing can happen for you if you defy the gravity that tends to pull us inward and downward in the third quarter.

◆ ◆ ◆

What does every football team do after the second quarter? It heads to the locker room to hit the pause button, reflect on what did or didn't work during the first two quarters, and then make the necessary adjustments. We can do the same thing.

◆ ◆ ◆

FOURTH QUARTER

In football, the fourth quarter carries a certain urgency. Time is running out. How are you going to finish? In life, the fourth quarter signifies old age. Unfortunately, too many people simply give up as they enter their seventies. Health issues may begin to play a role. Some of that is because our culture celebrates youth, relegating older people to anterooms of insignificance. The concept of the wise and revered "elder" that we see in many other cultures, especially Asian cultures, is absent in our own. But our elders bear at least some responsibility for their isolation. Gerontologist Ken Dychtwald's research shows that the average retired person watches 49.8 hours of television a week. I can't imagine a worse way to grow old.

My model for the fourth quarter is the story of former astronaut and senator John Glenn. *Time* magazine featured him on the cover of their August 17, 1998, issue for going back into outer space at the age of seventy-nine. Commenting on that achievement, he said, "Just because I am aging doesn't mean I stop having dreams." I love it and plan to keep on dreaming to the end, and I recommend you do the same.

Success in our first three quarters is measured in terms of things we can see: cars, boats, homes, and so on. In the fourth quarter, success is measured by things we can't see: honor, integrity, and respect. It is a time when we tend to lose power (there's no fancy title on your business card) but gain influence. Look at Jimmy Carter, who once held the most powerful office in the world but has probably had more influence on the world while in his seventies and eighties than during his four years as president of the United States.

We often think of our later years—the fourth quarter—as a time to rest, to take it easy: "I'd love to sail around the world, but I'm too old." "Too old" is a phrase I'd like to banish from our collective vocabularies. The next time you grab a bucket of chicken at KFC, remind yourself that Colonel Sanders started that successful chain when he was sixty-seven years old. At eighty-three, Michelangelo was still creating at Saint Peter's Basilica. Distance-runner Paul Spangler finished his fourteenth marathon when he was ninety-two years old. We often let our culture's take on old age become our own, missing out on opportunities for joy and adventure that can continue right up to our final moments on this planet.

Understanding the stages of life helps us develop a cadence or dance with life. In the first quarter we learn to hurry, to grab life with gusto, and that's a great way to begin the game. But by the time we enter the locker room, we've taken a few hits and need to sit back, take a deep breath, and reflect. Doing so prepares us for the remainder of the journey, allowing us to almost detach from ourselves and watch the seasons of life unfold. It's almost like watching a movie of your own life...

This brings me back to Sister Camille and football.

At the University of Wisconsin, after each football game— won or lost—the marching band comes out on the field and plays

"You've Said It All" (the Bud song) as the fans rise to their feet and dance, sing, drink, and celebrate. Win or lose. It's the fans' way of expressing gratitude for the game. They call it the fifth quarter, and it's a fitting finale to a great day.

One day I was talking to Sister about the four quarters of life, and she asked me what quarter she was in. Sister Camille is ninety-four years young. She told me that when she wakes up every morning, she is so grateful to live at the retirement center with the other Franciscan nuns. In her heart, she sings and dances, celebrating life itself. I love attending Mass with her and the other nuns, often staying for dinner. Of course, I'm not allowed to visit unless I bring a case of wine.

Sister Camille is in the fifth quarter of life, and if we should be so lucky to live into our nineties, we can experience that same gratitude for life itself.

Go to the Tape

1. If the game of life is divided into four quarters, what quarter are you in right now? What are the most important challenges you are experiencing in this quarter of your life?
2. How is the quarter you are in different from the previous quarter?
3. Conventional wisdom suggests that you will retire sometime in your early- to mid-sixties. What do you plan to be doing in your sixties?
4. What "dreams" do you have that you someday hope to achieve? What are the barriers to those dreams?
5. If you are given a lifetime achievement award when you turn ninety, what would you want it to be for?

CHAPTER 8

Strength Comes from Others— the Value of Great Guides

◆ ◆ ◆

To paraphrase Sir Isaac Newton, we lead longer,
healthier, and more prosperous lives because
we stand on the shoulders of giants.

—CHRIS LOWNEY, *HEROIC LIVING*

ALL GREAT PLAYERS—ALL GREAT COACHES—ALWAYS have this response whenever they're interviewed after a great performance: "I couldn't have done this without the help of..." Running backs credit their offensive lines. Wide receivers remind us that someone had to throw those passes accurately. Coaches point to general managers, owners, and others. They all recognize one of the most important truths about greatness: you seldom achieve it on your own.

◆ ◆ ◆

We all need heroes. Heroes remind us of what
we can all be, while inspiring us to grow.
—Jon Leonetti

◆ ◆ ◆

I've found this to be true in the business world as well. Some of the most powerful and influential leaders I've known are quick to acknowledge that much of their success has come from the hard work and wisdom of others. David Ogilvy, who is considered to be the father of modern advertising, once said, "If you ever find a man who is better than you are, hire him. If necessary, pay him more than you would pay yourself." He also once gave each member of his board of directors a set of Russian dolls. When they eventually got to the smallest doll, it had a piece of paper folded inside on which Ogilvy had written, "If you always hire people who are smaller than you, we shall become a company of dwarfs. If, on the other hand, you always hire people who are bigger than you, we shall become a company of giants."

Here's a guy who led one of the most successful advertising agencies—a business loaded with big egos—basically acknowledging that his strength comes from others.[2]

I suspect you already know that one of the keys to living a life filled with meaning and purpose is the kind of wisdom and truth telling that comes from two popular sources: mentors and guides or accountability partners. Mentors are generally older individuals, seasoned by experience and generous enough to share what they have learned. Accountability partners tend to be friends or colleagues about your own age who care about you enough to tell you the truth, even if it hurts. Or, as a friend of mine puts it, they will

---

2 David Ogilvy, *The Unpublished David Ogilvy* (London: Profile Books, 2014), 137.

not hesitate to give you the "unvarnished reality." At the very least, you need at least one of each in your life right now. But is that enough? After further reviewing my own life, I realized I needed more and landed on a unique concept that has proven invaluable to me: my virtual board of directors.

I'm sure you're familiar with the way companies and nonprofits appoint or elect people with expertise or experience to serve as members of their boards of directors. They establish these boards for the purpose of guiding their businesses or organizations to success. The board is usually organized around committees that specialize in specific areas key to the organization's growth and development. The primary beneficiary is the CEO, who has all this collected wisdom at his or her disposal. The CEO would never think of making a major decision without first running it by the board and listening carefully to its input.

Over the course of my career, I've served on twenty-eight boards and currently sit on six. I've seen how much of a difference a good board of directors can make to the success of the organization and began to wonder if I could recruit my own board to advise me on life issues. I mean, if boards are so critical to an organization's success, why not have our own boards?

Because it's challenging. It's difficult enough to find someone willing to mentor you or serve as your accountability partner. Putting together a board of really talented and experienced people to serve as a board just for *me*? That'll never happen. Or could it? In this age of virtual reality, *anything* can happen, including having Abe Lincoln serve on my board of directors, but I'm getting ahead of myself.

From my experience of serving on boards and understanding how they are structured, I began to dream a little. What if

I formed committees for the areas of my life that, after further review, are important to me and then began looking for the best people to serve on those committees? I mean the very best. Forget about their availability. I'll deal with that later. I formed these six committees:

Leadership
Marketing
Business
Spirituality
Training and Development
Aging Gracefully

Next, I began "recruiting" board members for each of these committees, and to do so I borrowed a practice from my childhood that I referred to earlier. Every time my buddies and I hit the backyard gridiron, we pretended we were one of the greats from past NFL teams. What we were really doing was copying—or at least trying to copy—the qualities that made them great. I know, we're not supposed to copy, right? When you copy from one person, it's called plagiarism; copy from a bunch of people, and we call it research. But when I took the snap from center as Bart Starr, I was trying to emulate his ability to scramble under pressure and throw a strike on a rope to Boyd Dowler.

Why not do the same thing for my board of directors—find people with expertise in the various areas represented by my committees and then try to copy or emulate them? The cool thing about this is that you can put virtually anyone on your board. Thus the term "virtual board of directors."

◆ ◆ ◆

At times our own light goes out and is rekindled
by a spark from another person. Each of us has
cause to think with deep gratitude of those
who have lighted the flame within us.
—Albert Schweitzer

◆ ◆ ◆

I started by recruiting legendary UCLA basketball coach John
Wooden. He agreed! OK, in my dreams, but that's what makes
your virtual board of directors possible. You really can have the
board of your dreams, and what better place for me to start than
with a guy who's won ten NCAA championships? His success as
a leader of young men was enough to qualify him to serve on my
leadership committee, but as I learned more about him, I was pro-
foundly struck by the fact that his number one trait as a coach and
as a person was humility. If anyone had the "right" to have a big
head or feel self-important, it would be Coach Wooden. But everyone around him reported that he truly was a humble man. He once
said, "Humble people don't think less of themselves, they just think
of themselves less." Humility is a trait I wanted in my life, and by
having him on my board, I now have a strong leader who can teach
me humility. I know this may sound strange, but whenever I feel
myself getting too big for my britches—getting all wrapped up in
what I'm accomplishing—I can actually go to him, virtually, and
ask, "Coach, give me the strength and power of humility." There
are a lot of ways I can go to Coach Wooden. I can (and do) read
his books. I can think about him, google him, and read his inspirational quotes or stories about how he interacted with his players.

Having Coach Wooden on my board and being able to call on him in this area has been transformative for me. Often as I've worked on this book, I've had to go to Coach and ask him to keep me humble. It gives me the feeling of connecting with a senior partner. In fact, remember that "What Would Jesus Do?" fad? In this situation, I changed it to WWWD—"What Would Wooden Do?"

I've also always been a huge fan of the leadership style of President Ronald Reagan, so I put him on my leadership committee. (How many corporations boast an ex-president on *their* boards?) I especially liked the way Reagan used humor. Despite being the most powerful leader in the free world at a time when the threat of a communist Soviet bloc still made people nervous, he tamed many tense situations with his wit and funny stories. As in the time he was shot by John Hinkley Jr. With a bullet lodged inches from his heart, as he was wheeled into surgery, he smiled up at his medical attendants and quipped, "I hope you're all Republicans." Or in the face of concerns that he was too old to run for president, he responded, "Just to show how youthful I am, I plan to campaign in all thirteen states." That's the kind of leader I want to be, so why not learn from and emulate the best?

Over a period of time, I recruited a total of thirty-six extraordinary people to serve on my virtual board of directors. Just as traditional board members are vetted or checked out to see if they can make a significant contribution, I read everything I could get my hands on that was either written about them or that they wrote themselves. For example, I've read every book written by Wayne Dyer, the internationally known speaker and writer on the general area of self-improvement, which has turned me into a huge fan. Thus, he sits on the training-and-development committee of my board. From reading practically everything written by Fr. Richard

Rohr, a Franciscan priest, I knew he was someone who should sit on my board's spirituality committee.

◆ ◆ ◆

Imagine having your own world-class board of directors available any time, night or day.

◆ ◆ ◆

At the end of this chapter I'll introduce you to each of my board members, but it's less important that you know who they are than what I actually do with my board. It's one thing to create your board of directors, but just having a list of names isn't going to do much for you. Some companies—especially nonprofits—make a big deal about creating a board, but then they virtually ignore it. Those organizations often fall into disarray and seldom carry out their mission effectively. The whole point of having a board is to benefit from the collective wisdom of its members. Because I'm a visual guy, I knew I needed some type of physical representation of my board—something that would keep them in front of me. I hired someone to arrange my board in a visually attractive piece of framed art that hangs in my office at home and at work. Whenever I walk past it—which happens several times a day—I'm reminded that I'm not alone, that I have thirty-six remarkable people whose qualities I can emulate and whose stories contain the wisdom I need to grow. But even that's not enough. As with any board, the CEO or leader needs to be able to pick up the phone and call a board member and ask for help whenever it's needed. Which is sort of what I do.

First, I begin every morning with a board meeting during my time of quiet reflection. I go over every name on my board and reflect on his or her qualities and how I will deliberately try to live them out that day. I look at Saint Teresa of Calcutta and remind myself that I want to be kind and loving to others, especially to the poor and downtrodden. I look at Holocaust survivor, Joe Demler, who lives by the words "every day is a bonus," and I make a conscious decision to live today as if it were the last day of my life. This daily board meeting inspires me to live the way I really want to live rather than fit in to someone else's expectations. It keeps me centered throughout the day, reminding me I'm not alone—that there are others who have set high standards and lived up to them.

I also "consult" with various board members when I run into a problem or challenge that threatens to drag me down. For example, as I was working on this chapter, I was struggling with a personal issue, so I went to four of my board members who I knew had experienced similar issues and asked them for guidance. It's not like I heard some spooky voice from the grave or anything weird, but by focusing on them in light of what I was dealing with, I was able to clearly see how to successfully resolve the issue. It's like those times when I emulated Bart Starr. I took on his qualities, wore them as if they were my own, and that's what I do when I consult with my board members.

How to Form Your Own Board

I'll admit that thirty-six board members might be a bit over the top, so don't let the numbers deter you from forming your own board. Some people I know have created boards with only three or four members. Others have ditched the whole idea but instead regularly read about the lives of great people they'd like to emulate. This is really a practice of allowing yourself to grow from the wisdom and experience of others. The important thing is, as that shoemaker says, to "just do it."

Start by creating the committees for your board. What are the three to six areas or components that you want to grow in your life? The ones I chose are specific to me and may not be ones that you would choose. That's OK. One way to get at this is to ask yourself, "What are the parts of my life that contribute to the whole?" For example, if you're an entrepreneur, you may value innovation. Make that one of your committees. Or maybe you're the type of person who's brimming with creativity, but in order to actually create something, you need discipline. Form a discipline committee.

Once you have your committees, begin the recruiting process. Who in all of history would be the best people to serve on each committee? If, for example, you have an innovation committee, who are some of the most innovative people you've ever heard of? It doesn't have to be someone from ancient history, but it should preferably be someone with whom you are familiar. Try to select at least three members for each committee, and for each member identify a specific quality that you admire (see my board below).

After you've assembled your board, use it. You may not want to follow my example by calling a daily board meeting, but find the best way for you to consult with your board regularly. Learn as much as you can about each of them, with the goal of trying to let their best qualities influence yours.

One final thought about benefiting from the wisdom of others: creating your virtual board of directors shouldn't replace the need for mentors and accountability partners. There's still something powerful about face-to-face meetings with individuals who will take the time to speak into your life. It's just that the busyness of life sometimes makes it difficult to have those meetings. Having a world-class board of directors supplements those meetings, and it's available any time, night or day.

As a kid, whenever I used to imagine myself as one of my sports heroes, I never actually became as good as any of them. But by copying the way they stood in at the plate, ran a post pattern, or head faked past a defender, I got better. A lot better. That's the whole point of emulating the qualities you admire in others. It reminds you who and what you want to be and inspires you to grow into that person.

As promised, here's my board, along with a brief explanation of why I recruited these members. After reviewing it, start creating your own.

LEADERSHIP

1. Ronald Reagan—fortieth president, used humor to overcome political divisiveness
2. Abe Lincoln—sixteenth president, how to overcome adversity and have a positive outlook when things get dark
3. John Wooden—the value of humility
4. Matthew Kelly—Catholic thought leader, working tirelessly to help others become best versions of themselves
5. Charles Krauthammer—political commentator, demonstrates value of common sense in all aspects of life, not just politics
6. Mr. Rogers—the value of kindness and unconditional love

MARKETING

7. Jim Fitzgerald—Wisconsin businessman, former owner of Milwaukee Bucks and Warriors, businessman's mind with an Irishman's heart

8. Bob Harlan—former CEO and president of the Green Bay Packers, value of connection with people
9. Lou Holtz—coached for Notre Dame and analyst at ESPN, value of goal setting, self-deprecation, and humility
10. Joe Demler—former World War II veteran/POW, value of gratitude, every day is a bonus

BUSINESS

11. Ned Bechthold—how to enjoy life the right way, all-around great businessman to emulate
12. Ab Nicholas—chairman of Nicholas Funds, the art of giving back
13. Steve Jobs—art of innovation and anticipating future needs
14. Bob Buford—Texas businessman, author, how to look forward to second half of your life, reframed my life from success to significance
15. Henry Ford—vision, industrious and enterprising, creating value for others
16. Edison, Firestone, and Harding—hard work, creativity, and foresight

SPIRITUALITY

17. Saint Ignatius of Loyola—founder of the Jesuit order; motto, "We're here to be men and women for others"
18. Saint Teresa of Calcutta—taught us to see God and the divine in everyone we meet

19. Jesus—loved and believed so strongly, He was willing to die for us

20. Sister Camille—continues to exemplify the value of gratitude, how to create grace-filled moments in every encounter of our lives

21. Saint Francis of Assisi—founder of Franciscan order, modeled networking, business, and how life is about giving and not receiving

22. Lao Tzu—spread the wisdom from his work, the *Tao Te Ching*

23. Buddha—wisdom figure on caring for all creation

24. Thomas Merton—Catholic thought leader, preached the value of contemplation and reflection

25. Fr. Richard Rohr—Franciscan priest, helped me to understand and try to live Franciscan philosophy

TRAINING AND DEVELOPMENT

26. Abraham Maslow—father of positive psychology, understands self-actualization, becoming a self-actualized person

27. Wayne Dyer—the art of manifestation in your life

28. Jack Canfield—inspirational speaker and trainer, personal coach

29. Carl Jung—combined worlds of psychology and spirituality better than anyone and how they work together

30. Joseph Campbell—mythologist, author, and teacher of how life is a hero's journey

31. Neville Goddard—metaphysical thought leader, imagination creates reality

Aging Gracefully

32. Michelangelo—aging gracefully, never too old to do anything
33. Bob Hope—died at one hundred, served others right up until end of his life
34. George Burns—humorist, demonstrated how to look forward to things as we grow old
35. Jack LaLanne—a picture of explosive energy throughout entire life
36. Paul Newman—created companies in his second half of life whose profits go to charity, realized the importance giving back

Go to the Tape

1. What three areas of your life are important to you? Health and wellness? Finances? Leadership? Education? Contribution to community?
2. Who are the experts or guides for you in those areas? Find three great people who displayed great discipline. Who are three great innovative people you could learn from?
3. What daily ritual can you create to continue a connection with these people throughout the day?
4. What books and research can you read to get closer to these people and learn more about them?
5. In addition to your virtual board of directors, who are your accountability partners and mentors whom you can meet with in person?

6. In what areas of your life are you most vulnerable for failing to live up to your expectations? What is your Achilles' heel? How might an accountability partner help you rise above these areas?

CHAPTER 9

Who? Why? Asking Great Questions

◆ ◆ ◆

What people think of as the moment of discovery
is really the discovery of the question.

—JONAS SALK

ONE OF MY ALL-TIME FAVORITE sports movies is *Hoosiers*, starring Gene Hackman and Dennis Hopper. As the title suggests, the movie takes place in a small southern Indiana town. At the time, Indiana was one of a few states that didn't match up sports teams based on the size of the schools, making it possible for a tiny, rural school to go up against a big-city school, which is the story line of *Hoosiers*. A ragtag bunch of farm kids make it all the way to the state finals, where they meet South Bend, the obvious favored team, with its much taller and athletic players.

When Hackman, the new coach, arrives, he addresses the entire town of about 153 people: "The boys and I are getting to know one another. We are trying to figure out who we are and who we want to become." He articulates what great coaches frequently and regularly ask of their teams—not how many games are we going to win, or where will we place in our division. But who are we?

Back in the day, under Woody Hayes, Ohio State's football team was known as a "three-yards-and-a-cloud-of-dust" run-it-down-your-throat offense. Today's New England Patriots, under Coach Bill Belichik, has established its identity as a precise, attention-to-every-detail operation (including that little detail about pounds per square inch—"deflategate"). In fact, name any great team in any sport, and avid sports fans would likely be able to describe that team in an adjective or two. However, teams that routinely languish in the cellar lack that clear, distinctive identity that we see in winners.

When I was much younger, I thought I had to have all the answers. But after further review of what's really important in life, I now recognize that asking the right questions is a lot more important than knowing all the answers. In fact, as I've studied the lives of people I truly admire, I've found that they were more interested in questions than in answers. For example, during the 1950s, a frightening polio epidemic swept through the United States. In 1952, fifty-eight thousand new cases of polio were reported, killing more than three thousand and leaving some twenty thousand seriously debilitated or paralyzed. With no known cure, scientists began a race to find some way to stop the spread of this growing health crisis. Eventually, a scientist by the name of Jonas Salk discovered a vaccine that eventually led to the eradication of polio *worldwide*. Here's what he said about his quest for a vaccine. "What people think of as the moment of discovery is really the discovery of the question." In other words, the only way he could come up with the answer to this disease was to discover the right question.

Asking the right questions is critical in sports. In science. In business. And in life.

So what exactly are the right questions? Vice Admiral James Stockton knew. In the 1992 presidential election pitting Bill

Clinton against George H. W. Bush, a third party emerged, led by Ross Perot and his vice-presidential candidate, James Stockton. In a nationally televised debate between the candidates for vice president, Stockton introduced himself by asking two questions: "Who am I? And why am I here?" Unfortunately, as the candidates began to debate, it was painfully obvious that Stockton didn't really know much about the issues of the day, and by the end of the debate, he came off sounding like a political lightweight. But all the late-night comedians focused on was the "who-am-I, why-am-I-here" questions. If Perot had even a slight chance at winning, Stockton's debate performance hurt the campaign.

The truth is, Stockton raised two of the most important questions any of us can ask, but it wasn't until several years later that we all recognized why he raised them. Appearing on a talk show in 1999, he acknowledged he felt terrible about his performance in the debate because he never got the opportunity to explain the logic behind those questions. He then went on to explain that he spent four years in solitary confinement in Vietnam, and a total of seven and a half years as a prisoner of war. Through all the pain, suffering, and isolation, he reflected on his experiences, and it changed his whole perspective and his sensitivity to life, giving him a new vision of what it meant to be an American. A powerful story began with just two questions.

◆ ◆ ◆

Asking the right questions is a lot more important than knowing all the answers.

◆ ◆ ◆

We live in an age of answers. Google "best restaurants in the United States," and you'll get 175 million answers in 1.23 seconds. But none of those answers are more important than these two questions: Who am I? Why am I here?

WHO AM I? WHY AM I HERE?

A while back, I was meeting with a group of businesspeople in Milwaukee. One of the guys asked, "Hey, Sweeney—I see you're writing books and doing a lot of speaking. I thought you were a hard-charging entrepreneur and investment banker. What's going on?"

At the time, I was making a deliberate shift in my career that better reflected the things that really mattered to me. While I was pretty excited about this new direction, it was uncharted territory, and I was little unsure of where it would take me. And given my terminal insecurity, it felt like my business peers were calling me out—challenging my business chops, even implying I wasn't the big shot I used to be.

I took the bait.

"Well, as you know, I've always enjoyed doing a lot of different things, like the time I spent as a sports agent representing three-time MVP Brett Favre. And I'm still involved in five private equity investments and sit on five corporate boards."

Later that evening, as I got in my car to drive home, I reflected on the evening, and all I could think was what a pathetic character I was. Instead of owning up to this exciting new turn in my life, I had just defined myself on what I used to do and what I still owned. I was more concerned with what they thought of me than who I was as a human being. Yet a lot of us do that all the time. We either try to be something other than who we truly are, or we define ourselves by what others think of us. Neither of those options represents your true identity, and we'll never discover that authentic person if we keep asking the wrong questions. For example, consider these questions that we either ask ourselves or that are asked of us:

* What do you want to be when you grow up?
* Where do you plan to go to college?
* Are you ever going to get married?
* When are you going to give us a grandchild?
* What are your salary requirements?
* What was your average income over the last three years?
* How much do you think you will need in retirement?

Important questions? You bet! But as you answer them and many more like them that will come your way, consider spending some time thinking about who you really are and why you're here. Knowing that will make it easier for you to answer all the other questions that you will face throughout your life.

◆ ◆ ◆

I had just defined myself on what I used to do and what I still owned. I was more concerned with what they thought of me than who I was as a human being.

◆ ◆ ◆

Knowing who you are and why you're here really go hand in hand, for as psychologist Susan Krauss Whitbourne explains, a strong identity emerges from a conscious contemplation of your life's purpose. In other words, essential to knowing who you are is understanding why you're here. OK, that just sounded like a pile of psychobabble, so let's try to translate what I just wrote into real life with an exercise I encountered at a Jesuit silent retreat. This is a long process, but it will help you to begin the process and get started...

1. Write down your parents' full names, birthplaces, and birth dates. How many siblings did each have? Describe each of your parents—what are their dominant traits? What adjectives would you choose to describe them?

2. Now focus on yourself. Write down your full name and when and where you were born. Write down your gender, race or ethnic group, religion—even details like your hair color (if you have any left), eye color, and physical build. Do the same for each of your siblings. List every place you've lived—the name of the city and a description of your house or apartment.

3. List six-to-eight personal characteristics or qualities that you feel you inherited from your parents and the way you were nurtured. For example, if your father was generous, did you inherit that quality from him? Another way to look at this is to describe how you are like your father or mother.

4. Now look a little deeper at yourself. What do you like about yourself? What qualities or traits give you the greatest sense of satisfaction or even pride?

5. What don't you like about yourself? What are some qualities or traits that you would change if you could?

6. What are you good at? What skills or knowledge do you have? What contributions to others do you make that you enjoy doing? What do you feel called or inspired to do that goes beyond a career or a job?

Write all of this down, and over the next several weeks, set aside some time to read through your answers, and as you do, begin crafting your answer to the two basic questions: Who am I, and why am I here? For example, as I went through this exercise, I wrote down that my mom was extremely gregarious and cared deeply about others, while my dad possessed a strong work ethic and had a kind, generous, and loving heart. I probably knew that intuitively, but seeing it in black and white helped me develop a clearer understanding of my own identity. When I listed all my siblings—nine—and first cousins—fifty—I realized that I've always been connected to a larger group. The exercise also helped me identify those things about myself that I liked—that I'm outgoing, generous, ambitious, caring, and athletic—as well as those things I wanted to change: I'm impatient, insecure, and judgmental.

By the time I finished reflecting on all that I had written down, I was able to clearly and accurately answer those two basic questions:

Who am I? I am an energetic, caring, and connected person who loves to help others on their personal and professional journeys.

Why am I here? My intention and purpose is to inspire one hundred million people to do things they want to do but never thought they could do.

Create Space

When professional sports leagues began considering the use of instant replay to review close calls, just about everyone objected because it would slow down the game. And I think that's why we resist spending time on asking the right questions. It takes time. We've become so conditioned to *doing* that we've neglected what we are *being*. We're too busy to sit quietly and reflect on the right questions. Besides, it's a lot easier to just keep playing the game, even if we keep blowing the calls. But think about it. When you find your identity in what you do and what you have, what happens when you quit doing those things or lose what you have? This is why so many people—especially baby boomers—fall apart when they retire. Without a title, an office, a business card, and all the trappings of success, they have no idea who they are or why they're here. Maybe that's why more than seven million people over the age of sixty-five suffer from depression, and that same category of adults makes up 16 percent of all suicides annually.[3]

Asking the right questions takes time because the answers aren't always easy or obvious. Questions about identity and purpose and meaning push us into places that may be uncomfortable. For example, you may have had a difficult childhood; your parents may have had qualities that you don't admire. Even in the best of circumstances, not everything that has influenced us from our past is positive. My dad's work ethic could easily push him toward being a workaholic, and he had some habits that troubled me. But if we don't lean into those negative influences, we run the risk of letting them creep into our own identities. By reflecting on all that has shaped me, I'm able to see those areas where I have to be careful. I'm able to accept and grow those qualities that I admire and avoid the ones I don't.

◆ ◆ ◆

We're too busy to sit quietly and reflect on the right questions. Besides, it's a lot easier to just keep playing the game, even if we keep blowing the calls.

◆ ◆ ◆

---

3 http://www.healthline.com/health/depression/elderly-and-aging#Overview1

103

There's another downside to not asking the right questions, and I call it tribalism. We so want to belong that we identify ourselves by whatever group we find ourselves in. So instead of being Joe Sweeney, I'm Irish. Or Catholic. I'm a liberal. Conservative. Now, some of this is just harmless fun. I'm a Cowboys fan. You're a Lions fan.

But once we get past our sports rivalries, our tribalism becomes caustic and leads to the kinds of divisions that are tearing our nation apart. Not to simplify some of the real issues that divide people, but I believe a large part of that comes from not knowing who we are as human beings. We've lost that sense of belonging to this wonderful and diverse family of earthlings. Gone is the deep inner sense that each of us is a unique individual loved by God. It is only when we know and are comfortable with who we are and why we're here that we are able to accept one another on the basis of our truest selves rather than whatever tribe we happen to belong to. I love the way Winston Churchill put it. "When there is no enemy within, the enemies outside cannot hurt you." Knowing who you are, then, is not only essential to your own ability to live an authentic, purposeful life, but it frees you from the bondage of trying to be what everyone else expects you to be.

All this from asking the right questions.

Go to the Tape

In addition to the questions I addressed in this chapter, here are some that will lead to more purpose and meaning in your life.

1. In terms of what you want to accomplish in your life, where are you right now, where do you want to go, and what will it take for you to get there? Who can help you get there?

2. What do you value most in life, and how are those values reflected in the way you live?
3. What are the things in your life that you need to accept?
4. What are the things in your life that you need to change?
5. If you had to list only three adjectives that best describe who you want to be, what are they? How accurately do those adjectives describe you?
6. What gives you joy? What could you do to experience more of it?
7. What is your wildest dream, and what are you doing to turn it into reality?

CHAPTER 10

Living Your Legacy–Going on Your Journey

◆ ◆ ◆

EACH YEAR, 1,696 FOOTBALL PLAYERS suit up in the National Football League. Every starter hopes to have a breakout season—the kind of regular performance that gets him on the cover of *Sports Illustrated*, a spot on the all-pro lineup, maybe even get in the running for most valuable player. And if he can sustain that level of excellence over his entire career, there's a chance he might get voted into the NFL Hall of Fame. It is at that point that we begin talking about that player's legacy.

When I think of legacies in the NFL, I recall greats like Bart Starr, Roger Staubach, and Joe Montana. In other professional sports, names come to mind like Michael Jordan, Gordie Howe, or Robin Yount. These are individuals who left their mark on the game by consistently doing all the right things and doing them exceptionally well. And you know what? None of them sat down with a few years left before retirement and decided they needed to work on their legacies. Their legacies began when they first started playing the game.

If you want to leave a legacy, you have to *live* a legacy.

When I was in my twenties, I didn't think much about my legacy. Who does at that age? In fact, it's usually not until we hit our middle years that we even consider the fact that someday we will be gone, and then what? How will I be remembered? What will I leave for my kids that has lasting value? I'm not talking about a will—my buddies keep reminding me I started with nothing, and I still have most of it left.

If you're under forty, you probably aren't too concerned about your legacy, and that's OK. You're likely right in the thick of things with work and family, which actually has a lot to do with legacy. You're sort of working on your legacy on autopilot. Hang in there, do your best, and eventually those teenagers will actually start liking you again.

If you're ninety, it's probably a little late to start working on your legacy. But you'll still leave one. If you beat up old ladies and stole money from your parish, it won't be a good one. More than likely, you've lived a good life and will leave the kind of legacy I hope to leave someday. Congratulations!

But here's the good news for the rest of us. Thanks to the fact that we're all living longer and healthier, at age fifty you will likely have another thirty years or more to live the kind of life that will have a lasting and positive impact long after you leave this earth. The question for you is this: "What can I do over the next thirty years that will be remembered and treasured for the following two hundred years?"

Here's a little hint: consider others.

Most of the great wisdom from various sacred texts suggests that we are at our best when we invest our time, talent, or treasure into others. Jesus invites us to feed the hungry, clothe the naked, and care for the widows and orphans. In Judaism, *tzedakah* is the Hebrew word for the acts that we sometimes call charity: giving aid, assistance, and money to the poor and needy and to other worthy causes. Some in the Jewish community say that this is the highest commandment in their religion. The Muslim Koran teaches that the highest form of devotion is to serve others, especially those in need. In Buddhism, the ideal practice or way of life is to selflessly act to alleviate suffering wherever it appears. If all wisdom comes from God—which I believe it does—we would be wise to live our legacies by pouring ourselves into others.

Have you ever attended a funeral in which the eulogies praised the deceased for how much money he had, the fancy cars he drove, or the exquisite outfits she wore? Instead, we usually hear about the great things the departed individual did for others.

* He was the kind of neighbor who, if I needed help with anything, would drop what he was doing and come help me.
* When I was in college, she wrote me a letter every week and always put a ten-dollar bill inside it. I can't tell you how encouraging that was.
* He's the main reason I made it through medical school. He made me believe in myself.
* Every time he bought his lunch at my sandwich shop, he always asked about my kids and left a tip far bigger than he needed to.
* I don't ever recall him complaining, but instead he always seemed to find the best in others and in every situation.

I'd rather leave a legacy like that than have my name plastered on the side of some building. Those kinds of comments are earned by the way you live day to day because your life is a journey that provides you with hundreds of opportunities that contribute to the legacy you will leave. And you don't have to live a charmed life or always be successful in order to leave a positive legacy. In fact, it's often through the way we respond to the disappointments—even failures—that form the building blocks of our legacies.

◆ ◆ ◆

What can I do over the next thirty years that will be remembered and treasured for the following two hundred years?

◆ ◆ ◆

In his book *Falling Upward,* Richard Rohr explains that when we experience pain in our lives, we have two choices. We can transform that pain into something good by learning and growing from it, or we can transfer it to others. For example, during my life I've been acquainted with my share of people who struggle with alcohol. Sadly, quite a few never got control over their drinking and allowed it to ruin their lives, their families, and their careers. We've all seen what I call the "bad alcoholic." They just resign themselves to their condition. He's the guy who shows up at his kid's basketball game drunk. Can't make it home from work without stopping for a few drinks on the way. Then comes a DUI, the last straw for his wife. The divorce triggers even more drinking. You know what I'm talking about. How tragic for a son or daughter to be left with a legacy like that: "I love my dad, but he was just another drunk." Your legacy is how you will be remembered after you're gone, and in that respect, we all will have a legacy. How sad to leave a legacy of disappointment and missed opportunities.

However, I've known those who have struggled with addictions and other problems rise above them. For example, I've watched a close friend face his addiction truthfully and courageously break its hold on him. It wasn't easy. In fact, it was incredibly embarrassing at first, like in that initial meeting with his recovery group: "Hi, I'm Dave, and I'm an alcoholic." Everything about his journey to sobriety took enormous humility, but guess what? He's been sober now for twelve years. He's still married, and his kids think the world of him. Two guys, two legacies. Which one would you want? One teacher says that when we experience pain or suffering, we can either lean into it and transform it into something positive or good, or we can ignore it and transfer it onto others. My friend leaned into his, and after he's gone, he will be remembered for the way he triumphed over a serious problem.

GOING ON YOUR JOURNEY

The Jesuits as an institution have created a great legacy of service to humankind. They understand the value of leaning into pain. As part of their novice experience, Jesuits are required to undertake a journey of uncertainty—usually to a city that is not familiar to them and with only a few dollars in their pockets. Thirty days on thirty dollars. No contacts at that city. No agenda other than to create an FUD experience: fear, uncertainty, and doubt. Because it is when we are tested with these emotions, we learn who we are and why we're here.

When I learned about the Jesuit novice journey, I decided I had to try it myself. With all that was going on in our cities, I felt I needed a new perspective on race, poverty, and violence, so on a hot summer day I boarded a Greyhound bus in Milwaukee and ended up in Detroit. And if you know anything about bus stations, you know that I walked off that bus and right smack-dab into the 'hood. Talk about fear, uncertainty, and doubt. My friends thought

I was nuts; my kids wondered if I was having a midlife crisis. But I had to do it. I actually felt called to do it.

◆ ◆ ◆

It's one thing to have convictions and beliefs, but what are you doing about them?

◆ ◆ ◆

I chose Detroit because I had spent about the last twenty-five years complaining about this place that President Lyndon Johnson allegedly predicted would be his legacy when he presented his policies. He mentioned looking to Detroit in fifty years, and calling it a shining light on the hill. Maybe my eyesight isn't as good as it once was, but when I stepped out onto Howard Street, I did not see a shining light on a hill.

But I did see a shining light, and his name was Alex.

About four blocks from the bus depot, I met Alex Cogswell, the first of many street people to ask me for money. Alex was enthusiastic, clean, and had a great smile. I liked him instantly and asked him what he needed money for. He said he was hungry and wanted to buy a burger.

"At six-thirty in the morning?" I asked skeptically and quickly was ashamed of myself when he answered.

"Yup. A nice juicy burger from Burger King."

We walked to the nearby fast-food joint and had a burger together, joined by about six of his friends.

Alex was like the mayor of the Detroit homeless community. He had a great personality, was polite, and I felt safe with him. I learned that he was the twelfth of twelve kids in his family and that he was schizophrenic. As long as he took the drugs provided for him by a local clinic, he was fine. But sometimes he forgot to take his drugs. I also learned that he had been homeless for eleven years. He gave me a tour of the downtown area, pointing out places where I could get some free food as well as places I should avoid.

"Don't sleep in the homeless shelters," he warned. "Lots of bedbugs, violence, drugs, and alcohol."

So where would I spend the night? He took me to where he lived, under a bridge near Joe Louis Arena. (The last time I visited the arena was with Craig Leipold, owner of the Minnesota Wild. We sat in a luxury box.) Alex had an extra sleeping bag that was dry and assured me that Charlie, who also lived there, wouldn't hurt us. He just drank too much.

I just couldn't get over how kind, generous, and friendly Alex was, and it caused me to rethink my attitudes about the homeless. He was genuinely concerned about my welfare, even though the "welfare state" wasn't working for him. He shared from what little he had. I know people with a lot who don't share like Alex did.

On that first day, I must have walked twenty miles. That's another thing you don't consider about the homeless. They don't have cars, and they certainly don't have money for cab fare or even public transportation. So they walk everywhere. I'm in pretty good physical shape, but all that pounding the pavement left me tired late in the afternoon, so I found a small park and stretched out on a bench to take a little nap. But almost as soon as I hit the bench, a security guard offered *his* version of welcome to Detroit.

"Take a hike—no sleeping in public parks."

I didn't have much money on me, but I found some. A quarter here. A dime there. A penny—twice! When I mentioned that to Alex, he told me that whenever he finds money—if even just a penny—he says, "Thank you, God, for all the abundance you have provided in my life."

I now do the same.

On my second day in Detroit, Alex took me to the stunningly impressive headquarters of General Motors. I think he was sort of proud of the architecture in his city and wanted to show it off. Alex couldn't have known this, but I am a part owner of Novum, the company that designed and manufactured GM's headquarters. He told me this is where the one-percenters worked, so I asked him what he meant by the one-percenters.

"They're the people who could afford an education, food, clothing, and houses."

To Alex and other people stuck in poverty, everyone else but them is a one-percenter.

One afternoon, Alex shared a little more on his thoughts about God. He told me he prayed this prayer every morning: "I will see God in everyone I meet today." He sounded a lot like Mother Teresa. He explained to me that the difference between the soul plane and spirit plane was the speed of the vibrations. The vibrations move faster on the spirit plane and slower and deeper on the soul plane. I thought, "Crap—this guy just explained something I couldn't answer for years!"

Alex also said he was trying to live God's will every day.

"If you live in God's will, you live under a divine umbrella."

It was raining when he said that.

Here I was, grimy and unshaven, talking with a homeless guy about some pretty deep beliefs. And what he said made so much sense, like his thoughts about material and spiritual gifts: your material gifts decrease when you give them away, but your spiritual gifts increase the more you use them. And get this one:

"When we are living in a conscious connection with God—this Divine Energy—you are one with him. In complete union with God. That is our greatest need—to overcome separation from one another and God. We need to realize that we are all connected by this thing called Divine Love."

Wow!

Finally, Alex ended our conversation by saying he was looking forward to the day that he could go home to God. I've gone to Mass all my life, and I've had the privilege of hanging out with a lot of religious leaders, but this conversation with Alex was a holy moment, one that I would have missed if I hadn't answered that nudge in my heart to step out of my comfort zone and into a world that I had always thought of as dirty and dangerous.

On my last day in Detroit, Alex and I stopped in at a Potbelly restaurant. I ordered a bagel for ninety-nine cents, and the guy handed me an extra one for Alex. I learned that a lot of fast-food joints and restaurants quietly take care of the homeless every now and then. We got a couple of glasses of water, sat down at a table to eat our bagels, and after we finished, I headed for the exit. I stopped, however, when I realized Alex was still at our table. He had gone back to the counter to grab some napkins and, using the water from his glass, spent the next few minutes scrubbing the table clean. I asked him why he did that, and his answer stunned me: "I always try to leave a place better than when I found it."

Alex may not know it, but he will leave a legacy. For one thing, I'll never forget him, and now you know about him, too. But I have a feeling that for a lot of people who have hit rock bottom, Alex brings hope and joy, a bright light in the dark alleys of Detroit. Not because one day he decided to "work" on his legacy, but because he is simply trying to be his best, connect with God, and help others regardless of his lot in life.

When I think about my own life, I like to think there are angels somewhere up there taking notes. If you don't believe in angels, here's another way to understand how you are building your legacy. Someone, somewhere is watching. Little that you do is unseen, especially by those closest to us. For example, what does your daughter think when she listens to you talk to your wife? What does your colleague think when you share a joke whose punch line comes at the expense of a minority? What does that stranger on the street corner holding out a little tin cup think when you walk past him without saying a word? All brief, seemingly insignificant actions, but your legacy is the sum of every one of them. A few years ago, I heard Mitt Romney speak, and this is what I remember most from his speech: "Our actions are words, and even the websites we browse all leave an impression in this book called your life. Whether we know it or not, every day we are writing the autobiography of our lives."

One of the keys to leaving the kind of legacy that I think we all want to have is to fight for those things that really matter to us. Ray Farley, former CEO of Johnson Wax, used to sit in meetings listening to his subordinates argue over things until he couldn't take it any longer.

"I find all of this *terribly* unimportant," he said, interrupting. "Let's move on."

We need to adopt that same attitude in our lives. It's one thing to have convictions and beliefs, but what are you doing about them? If you're just complaining about, for example, the sad state of public education, you're doing nothing more remarkable than the millions of others who are whining about it. Because complaining is being unhappy with a situation but being unwilling to do anything about it. So therefore, I'll just complain. How about volunteering to help kids learn to read in an inner-city classroom?

Or "adopting" a classroom teacher, learning more about the challenges he faces, and mobilizing others to get involved in their public schools? Those are the kinds of actions that create a legacy. Alex didn't just curse the darkness, but he actually lit a candle to bring some much-needed light to the problem. Fight for the values that stir your soul, and you'll leave a legacy that will inspire others for years to come.

After further review, you learn that all of life is fleeting—our health, our youth, and especially the things we've worked so hard to attain. It will all pass away. The only thing that lasts is your legacy. My new friend Alex, the homeless man from Detroit, offers all of us the best definition of that legacy—to leave everything we encounter better for the next person. Is your family better because of you? Is the team you lead at work better because of you? Is the young woman who served you at McDonald's better because you smiled at her or thanked her? Is the guy who picks up your trash having a better day today because you decided to get up early, wait by the curb, and thank him for the job he does?

◆ ◆ ◆

I always try to leave a place better than when I found it.
—Alex Cogswell

◆ ◆ ◆

Every day you have an opportunity to create a legacy so that in the end, anyone who ever had contact with you can say, "Life was better because of him."

What are you doing today—what will you do over the next ten, twenty, thirty years—that will have a positive impact and influence for generations to come?

Go to the Tape

ESPN Magazine runs a feature on the last page of each issue that chronicles "a day in the life" of a major sports figure. It's interesting, but it also offers a glimpse into the character, values, influences, rituals, et cetera, of that person. If it's true that in order to leave a legacy you have to live a legacy, how are you living on a day-to-day basis that will shape your legacy? Take some time to ponder and write down how you live a typical day. How does that measure up with the legacy you want to leave?

1. Write one full page entitled "A Day in the Life of Me"
2. What stories will people tell about you when you are gone?

CHAPTER 11

After You Leave the Game— The Art of Letting Go

◆ ◆ ◆

We shall not cease from exploration
And the end of all our exploring
Will be to arrive where we started
And know the place for the first time.

—T. S. ELIOT, "FOUR QUARTETS"

AT SOME POINT, IT'S TIME to go.

For most, it's not easy. Look at how difficult it is for professional athletes to leave the game. Often they hang on one year too long, leaving us with images of a once-great warrior barely able to keep up with his teammates. But it's not just athletes who find it difficult to let go. Few of us really look forward to retirement, and for good reason. The very word means to withdraw, fade away, or become less significant.

And yet, you can't keep doing what you're doing forever, so the issue is not if you should retire, but it's how you can let go in such a way that you can still enjoy a dynamic life of meaning and purpose. After further review, you will discover that there's a right way and a wrong way to leave the game.

As a former investment banker, I've worked with dozens of business owners who have lived the American dream. They started, built up, sold their businesses, and then "let go" the way a lot of wealthy people do: they pursued the "good life" of endless golf or cruises or travel. Sounds wonderful, right? To be able to do whatever you want, whenever you want. Except that method of letting go seldom ends well. I recall hearing about a guy who tracked down thirty-six men who had done just that—sold their businesses so they could live the rest of their lives in pursuit of leisure. The first three were devout Christians who loved God, loved their wives and families, and had a strategic plan to enjoy the fruits of their wealth. All three ended up with broken relationships within a year. His point in sharing this was to demonstrate that true happiness does not come in serving ourselves, but it comes through serving others. We think being able to do whatever we want to do will fulfill us, but it's an empty fantasy.

What if instead of thinking about retirement as a time to withdraw from your career and fade off into the sunset, we think of it as a time to *refire*? In other words, after you leave the game, find another way to play, whether it's volunteering, mentoring, or stretching yourself with a whole new career, albeit one you can play a little slower and with more enjoyment. Unfortunately, most of us are so driven—so hooked on the rush we get from our work—that we stay in the game longer than we should, and like the pro athlete who hangs on too long, we usually end up embarrassing ourselves.

So why is it so hard for us to let go? I've been blessed to have worked with and mentored a number of high-level business executives, professional athletes, and members of the elite navy SEALs. My work with them has mostly dealt with the topics of change and transition. What fascinates me is how these people can perform exceedingly well at such a high level, yet they struggle when it comes to periods of transition. What I've learned is that with all three groups, the struggle revolves around five common fears, and these fears likely afflict the rest of us as well:

1. The fear that your best years are over

If you've won the Super Bowl, set annual sales records, or rescued a fallen comrade behind enemy lines, what's to look forward to? Plenty, but it may not look exactly like those past accomplishments. What I tell these uberperformers is that they need to remember that those great accomplishments of the past stand as a testament to their ability to strive and achieve. As your own career winds down, let the memory of those "best years" propel you to even better years as you seek out the next adventure. Mike Golic, of ESPN's *Mike & Mike* radio show, used to be a defensive lineman for the Philadelphia Eagles. It's clear from listening to him that he'd love to be able to strap on the pads, grab his helmet, and spend Sunday afternoons terrorizing quarterbacks. But he left the game on his own terms and discovered he's pretty good at something else that he loves to do: talk sports every day with current and former athletes, sportswriters, and fans. And just for the record, I believe your best years are *always* ahead of you and are never over.

2. The fear you will never find anything as meaningful

When you are living and breathing continuous moments of meaning, adrenaline, and success, it can be difficult to imagine anything less, and letting go sure seems like less. It isn't. The fine art of letting go gives you the freedom to map out a new journey that will take you places you never dreamed of going. Will it be the same ride you've enjoyed for the past twenty-five to thirty years? No, and once you let that one go, you'll put yourself in a position to discover new opportunities for growth, service, and passion. I often recommend creating your own personal board of directors—wingmen or wingwomen, as I like to call them. These are people you trust and enjoy spending time with and whose opinions and expertise you value. Lean on them to help guide your decisions and provide recommendations that will open doors for your next adventure.

3. THE FEAR AND INSECURITY ABOUT FINANCES

When you're in the game, you get a regular paycheck. As you approach the time to leave the game, worries over money often convince you to keep playing, whether you're a professional athlete, business executive, navy SEAL, or whatever it is you do in your career, and for good reason. Take the professional athlete, for example. Yes, most make millions of dollars, but the average career in the NFL is 3.2 years. Many athletes spend big because they can, only to learn how quickly their finances can evaporate. If you think I'm exaggerating, check out the ESPN "thirty-for-thirty" film, *Broke*. You'll be amazed at how many big-name athletes who earned millions are literally broke.

Sadly, I know people who should be able to let go but did not make sensible financial decisions earlier in their lives. This is probably why we're seeing so many advertisements for companies that want to help you make sure you'll have enough money later in life. Instead of letting financial worries keep you in the game longer than you need to be, start making the kinds of decisions and choices that will give you the financial stability you need for the future—right now. This is the first time in recorded history that we worry more about living too long than about dying too young.

4. THE WORRY ABOUT LIFESTYLE

One of the most common questions I get from people approaching a transition is "What will I do the rest of my life?" My initial answer sort of startles them. "That's up to you." They—and we—are used to living a regimented life. You get up, go to work, come home, and go to bed. And you do it all over again tomorrow. On the one hand, you can't wait to get out of that rat race, but on the other hand, it's scary. Or as one guy said to me, what title do I put on my business card?

How about CIO—chief imagination officer? Dream big. You've got the rest of your life ahead of you. You don't have to go to those interminable meetings or call on accounts or solve a messy budget issue or do any of those things that have you pulling your hair out and waiting for the day you can walk away from all of that. Well, now's the time, and with a healthy imagination you finally can try something you never had the time or opportunity to do.

One little strategy that will help you determine how to spend the rest of your life is to create a "have-do-and-be" list. What do you need to have in order to do and be the person you want to be? For example, maybe you've always wanted to be a coach, but you never had the time to commit to that dream. One thing that you need to have to achieve that dream is time. When you finally let go, you'll have enough time to coach a Little League team or even help out with your local school or city recreation department. Creating a have-do-and-be list will make it easier for you to see what your ideal postwork life will look like as well as the steps you need to take to get there.

5. THE FEAR OF NETWORKING

By the time you're ready to let go, you've established a comfortable circle of friends and colleagues. You know some of these people as well as or better than your spouse. In many cases, you're not only an integral part of that circle, you're the center of attention. People look up to you and come to you for advice. And in return, you have a lot of go-to people in your corner, ready and willing to drop everything if you need help. If leaving that close-knit group is scary, trying to form new relationships that can help you negotiate the pathways to your next adventure can be downright horrifying. So you hang on just a little longer because it's so comfortable.

One way to overcome this fear is to think of networking as a place you go to give, not to get. You're not approaching someone with your hat in your hand, asking for something. Instead, you bring a lot of great experiences and wisdom to the table, and networking is a great way to share it. As you do, you will soon find your new network expanding, providing you with new relationships that will enrich your life.

THE ULTIMATE FEAR: DEATH

There's yet another fear that grips us and causes us to hold on as long as we can, a fear we don't like to talk about. I'm talking about the fear of dying. We divert our attention to it by working as long as we can, pretending we'll live forever. We won't. Ultimately, we all leave the game. For good. And the real art of letting go is learning how to die.

◆ ◆ ◆

After further review, you will discover that there's
a right way and a wrong way to leave the game.

◆ ◆ ◆

Whether our fears are related to letting go of our careers or the deeper
fear of dying, the real issue is that we have become so attached to
things that really don't matter: jobs, titles, possessions, money, security, and so on. The truth, however, is that we really don't own any
of this, including our bodies. We're only stewards of it for a while.
Eventually it all gets left behind, yet we are so attached to it that we
let it determine how we spend all our time and energy. That attachment leads us to fear loss, and the fear of loss is a stronger motivator
than the promise of a reward. In one psychological study, researchers
promised one group of children twenty dollars if they improved their
standardized test scores by a certain amount. Then they gave another group of children twenty dollars each on the condition that they
would lose that money if they did not improve their test scores. Guess
which group performed better? The second group, because they stood
to lose something they already had—they had become attached to the
idea of keeping that twenty dollars. Moral of the story? It's very easy to
become attached to things, even small things that don't matter much.

And much of what we are attached to are small things that
don't matter much.

The question remains for us: How do we detach from what we
know, what we do, and what we have? How do we detach from life
itself? As Fr. Richard Rohr reminds us in his book *The Art of Letting
Go*, we humans are the only species who struggle with death and
this detachment. Members of the animal or plant kingdoms never
struggle with or fear death because they're not attached to anything.

In fact, some animals readily accept and even invite death. For example, when a zebra herd is being chased by lions, the older zebras will deliberately slow down and allow the lions to kill them so that the younger ones can live. What a beautiful analogy to remind us that in our third and fourth quarters of life, one of our most important roles is to train and mentor those coming along behind us.

When we learn to live in the spirit of detachment, we learn to truly live. As Leonardo da Vinci once said, "When I thought I was learning how to live, I was really learning how to die." As I was working on this chapter, a friend of mine lost his brother to pancreatic cancer. As my friend shared about his brother, it was clear that his brother had learned to detach. He spent his last days not worrying about his possessions because he had already downsized and enjoyed the pleasure of giving things away and seeing the joy on the faces of friends and family who received these gifts of remembrance. While he loved life as much as anyone, he was not so attached to it that he fought the inevitable. He had lived his life in such a way that he was ready to go. Consequently, his friends and family observed his passing with more joy than sadness. That's what detachment does.

OK, that sounds good, right? Maybe even too good to be true. So how do you actually detach from the things you think are so important? At first, it's not easy. You start by recognizing what you're attached to. One of the things I realized I was attached to was my office—a beautiful penthouse suite on the twenty-eighth floor of Milwaukee's Kilbourn Tower, with glass walls offering a stunning view of Lake Michigan. To me, it was more than a kick-ass office; it defined who I was. It gave me a certain "swagger." In order to detach from this fallacy, I had to acknowledge how deeply I was attached to my office. I reminded myself that this beautiful creation of stainless steel, bricks, and glass is not me at all, and if it were, I would be a pretty shallow person.

Then I had to detach myself from that whole line of reasoning and accept the possibility of losing it, to recognize that it does not define me and that I don't need it to be a complete and whole person. I haven't canceled my lease, but if I had to move out tomorrow, I'm fine with it.

The final step in detachment is to attach to something of greater value. For me, that's God. But it could also be good people, good habits, good music, or good food, because in my opinion, what is truly good in this world is connected to God.

Here's another little trick to help you detach. One of the best features of a computer is the delete button, followed by the empty-trash button. Once you recognize and acknowledge what you are attached to, visualize yourself hitting the delete and empty-trash keys in your soul's computer. Start with the little things. For example, after further review, I realized that I was addicted to sugar. I generally eat a pretty healthy diet, but had I not reviewed my eating habits, I probably would not have learned just how attached I was to it. Now, whenever I find myself craving sugar, I imagine deleting that sugar-saturated snack and then detaching completely from it by clicking the empty-trash button. I even imagine hearing that "plunk" sound when it hits the bottom of the trash can. Before you call me crazy, try it. It works!

◆ ◆ ◆

When I thought I was learning how to live,
I was really learning how to die.
—Leonardo da Vinci

◆ ◆ ◆

And if you thought I was going off the deep end with the delete button, here's a detachment exercise that will likely certify me as crazy, but when you learn the art of letting go, you don't care. Each night as I fall asleep, I literally try to detach from my body and look down at myself from the ceiling. Give it a try. As you lie in your bed, imagine yourself relaxing every muscle and fiber in your body from head to toe. Then imagine your spirit rising up to the ceiling and looking down at your body. Wayne Dyer says we think we are physical beings with a spiritual component, but he tells us that in reality we're spiritual beings with a physical component—a component, I might add, that will eventually be gone. By trying to detach myself from my body, I remind myself of this eternal truth: our bodies fade away, but our souls or true essence as beings lives on forever.

The art of letting go is really learning to die every day. The Bible teaches in many different places that we are to die to ourselves (our egos) in order that we may be more fully present with God. To me, that means that letting go positions us for something better, something eternal. Richard Rohr puts it this way: "When we let go, we fall into God's merciful and loving presence, which paradoxically affirms our true power. Letting go is incredibly freeing and empowering!"

I began this chapter with this excerpt from T. S. Eliot:

We shall not cease from exploration
And the end of all our exploring
Will be to arrive where we started
And know the place for the first time.

I'm not a literary critic, but I believe Eliot was writing about dying. It brings to mind a journey that begins at birth and ends at the same destination, reconnected with the energy that sustains the universe. For most of our lives, we cling so tightly to things that we think will give us the satisfaction that we desire, but as we approach the finish line, we begin to have our doubts. Is this all there is? I worked so hard and so long for exactly what?

I heard a sermon once about a guy who was backpacking across Europe. One day he visited a rabbi who had offered to let him stay a few days. When the backpacker arrived, he was struck by the sparse furnishing inside the rabbi's house: just a small table, a few chairs, and no pictures on the wall or fancy drapes on the windows. Out of curiosity, he asked the rabbi why he had so little. Motioning toward the guy's backpack, he responded, "Just like you, I don't need much because I'm only going to be here for a little while."

After further review, the call on the field has been overturned. None of that matters as much as you think. It is only after you learn to detach yourself from all that you thought was so important that you will be free from your fear of death. I love life, but if I died tomorrow, I would die happy and content. When you daily practice the art of letting go, you are truly living.

Go to the Tape

1. Get rid of five things this week in your closet, your desk, and your garage. Repeat each month.
2. Try this simple exercise from Hale Dwoskin's "Sedona Method." Pick up a small, common object like a pencil or a stone. Grip it as tightly as you can until it becomes uncomfortable. Then open your hand. Is the object attached to your hand? What's preventing you from just letting it drop?

How is this much like the way you hold on to feelings, possessions, or relationships that are not helpful or healthy?

3. When you go to bed tonight, try looking down at yourself from the ceiling. What do you see? Someone who is brave, has followed his or her passions, was a good parent or spouse, took risks in relationships, and made a difference in the world?

4. Select a morning when you are free of any obligations—family, work, and community. Then find a quiet place where you will not be interrupted, and spend the morning thinking about your impending death.

CHAPTER 12

When to Call an Audible—New Tricks for the Playbook

◆ ◆ ◆

IF YOU'RE ANY KIND OF an NFL fan, you know who yelled out these words before the ball was snapped:

"Omaha, Omaha."

If you said "Peyton Manning," you know your sports trivia. You also know that he was calling an audible, changing the play at the last second because of something he saw in the defensive set. Maybe the cornerbacks were playing up close, signaling a possible blitz, or the defense was stacking the box, which would stop the run that he had called in the huddle. After "Omaha," he shouted out a few other code words, switching from a run up the middle to a quick pass to his slot receiver.

Sometimes you just have to mix things up in your life, and after further review, I've come up with four new "plays" that will help you play the game better.

THE VALUE OF HUMOR

Athletes are notorious for the pranks they pull on one another. My former client Brett Favre took advantage of the subzero weather in Green Bay to prank his teammates. He would get the keys to a player's car, start it up, and turn the air-conditioning on full blast, then pour water over the door and lock so that it froze shut. When the player finally was able to chip through the ice and get inside the car to warm his freezing hands, it was colder in the car than outside.

Peyton's little brother, Eli, is known as the "godfather of pranks" in the NFL. One of his best? He stole wide receiver Hakeem Nick's cell phone and punched a few keys, which switched the phone's language from English to Japanese. Then he quietly put the phone back into Hakeem's locker.

Chicago Cubs manager Joe Maddon has been dubbed by *Forbes* magazine as "the craziest manager of all time." Maybe it had something to do with bringing animals (like a penguin or boa constrictor) into the clubhouse—or making his entire team dress up as goofy nerds for a road trip. During one of his many heated arguments with an umpire, the official threatened to eject him if he said another word. "I love you," Maddon replied—and got tossed.

Are these just goofy guys who like to have fun? Probably, but with most sports pranksters, there's a method to their madness. Keep everyone loose. Take their minds off the game for a moment or two. It's a long, stressful season, and humor takes the edge off things.

To succeed in life you need three things:
a wishbone, a backbone, and a funny bone.
—Reba McEntire

◆ ◆ ◆

A little humor won't solve all your problems, but it sure makes your journey on this planet a lot more fun. And fun is good. If you haven't discovered it yet, life can be challenging. As you head off to work every day, have you ever wondered why they call it work? Because whatever job you have, it can at times take a toll on you. If you're in a leadership position, the decisions you make affect not just those who report to you, but their families, whether or not their kids can go to college, or what kind of vacation they can take. And if you report to that guy, you've got to bust your butt to make the numbers this month or finish that fifty-hour project in a forty-hour week. Then you go home, and even in the best families you have those days when you question all of the choices you have made.

I don't recommend cracking a joke when your spouse is upset with you or when your boss is getting on your case, but after the dust settles, a little laughter helps us all get through the rough spots that always come our way. Michael Kerr, author of *The Humor Advantage—Why Some Businesses Are Laughing All the Way to the Bank,* writes that humor not only is a great tension breaker in the workplace, but it actually produces better thinking. "People who laugh in response to a conflict tend to shift from convergent thinking where they can see only one solution, to divergent thinking where multiple ideas are considered."

Letting yourself enjoy a belly laugh once in a while might also be good for your health. The Old Testament declared that "A merry heart doeth good like a medicine." Back in the 1980s, popular author and magazine editor Norman Cousins was diagnosed with an incurable blood disease. As he wrote in *Anatomy of an Illness,* he watched Marx Brothers movies from his hospital bed and attributes that to beating the disease and living well into his eighties.

Scientists have learned that humor reduces pain, strengthens the immune system, and reduces stress.

The message here is that if you're a grouch, lighten up, and laugh a little. And if you enjoy a little mischievous fun, keep calling this audible, and everyone wins.

Humility

I've had the privilege of meeting some really well-known people, as well as a handful of the top business and thought leaders in the world. As I've gotten to know them and see all that they've accomplished, two things stand out. One is that they didn't get to where they are by accident. These men and women are smart, talented, and unafraid of hard work. But what surprises me most is how humble they are. Take Lou Holtz, for example, the former Notre Dame football coach and former ESPN commentator. He draws a crowd wherever he goes. He has to be one of the most recognizable and admired guys I've ever met. Even Michigan fans love him! Yet he's also one of the most humble guys I've ever met. When a fan approaches him for an autograph, he's more interested in them than they are with him. He talks to them and listens to what they have to say. And when a fan remarks about a particular great game from his coaching days, he's likely to respond with self-deprecating humor.

What exactly is humility, and why is it important? Joshua Becker, popular author and blogger at www.becomingminimalist.com, writes, "Humility is a funny thing. In fact, my grandfather used to tell us that he won a medal for his humility, but it was taken away when he began to wear it." In other words, if you have to tell people you're humble, you're probably not.

Richard Rohr defines humility as "a simple acknowledgement that I am very small, quickly passing, and insignificant as a separate self." What makes us who we are—what gives us dignity as humans—comes from our connection to God.

I have my own definition, one that I need to recite in front of the mirror every morning: you're not all that, so get over yourself. Too many of us believe our own press releases, forgetting that we're the ones who wrote them. Humility is the recognition that we're no better than anyone else, so let's start living as if we really believed that.

Consider some of these traits of a humble person:

* Puts others first
* Does not think too highly of himself or herself
* Listens to others
* Accepts criticism
* Admits mistakes
* Celebrates other people's achievements

If you want to have an influence on others, practice humility, because in an increasingly self-absorbed culture, it is the humble individual who will shine as a beacon. Whether you're a parent, Cub Scout leader, CEO of a major business, or manager of a fast-food joint, you will have more influence as a leader if you are truly humble.

Some people are naturally humble; most of the rest of us have to work at it. How? Every day we're given dozens of opportunities to practice. For example, consider your interactions with others, especially those who serve you or report to you. A simple "thank you," consistently offered, shows that you care about those people. That's humility. So is asking how they're doing and then listening.

When a colleague does something noteworthy, compliment her. Try to become that person who catches people in the act of doing something good. And if you screw up, own up to it; apologize.

Then repeat the next day.

SIMPLICITY

One thing I've noticed over my years as an athlete, sports fan, and sports agent is that the greatest teams have figured out the value of keeping things simple. Two examples come to mind.

Vince Lombardi, the legendary Green Bay Packer coach from the 1960s, developed an extremely simple play and put it in his team's playbook: the power sweep. Nothing fancy. Give the ball to the running back, and have him follow practically the entire offensive line around the end. Every team they played against knew it was coming, knew exactly where it was going, but couldn't stop it. Why? Because the Packers took something simple, practiced it religiously, and therefore executed it with perfection.

Then there was John Wooden, who was notorious for breaking the game of basketball down to its fundamentals—even to the point of taking the first day of practice each season to teach his players how to put their socks on. And why was this so important to the team's success? Put your socks on wrong, and you'll get a blister. Get a blister, and you may miss a game. Miss a game, and we lose your contribution to the team. We need you to win, so learn how to put your socks on.

Sometimes we make life more complicated than it needs to be. After further review, some days I just want to get rid of everything I own and start over. Maybe do that Walden Pond thing where I build a tiny cabin next to a lake and just enjoy nature. OK, that may never happen, but I think all of us at some point get overwhelmed with the complexity of our lives. We work so hard to have so much and then have to maintain it and find a place to put it. Our cell phones jar us regularly with beeps, reminding us of the next meeting, the next appointment, and the next soccer game. In our complex, always-on-the-go culture, a little simplicity may be just the ticket for helping you regain some clarity and purpose in life.

When I think of simplicity, I think of Mr. Rogers. One of the reasons kids loved him, I believe, is that he and his television show were so simple. Plain. Almost ordinary. He walked in every day, took off his coat and shoes, put on that cardigan and a pair of slippers, and then retrieved a package from Mr. McFeeley, the delivery man. Where other kids' shows exploded with action and noise, *Mr. Roger's Neighborhood* was calm and quiet. And despite the various characters and scenes, his message was always the same. Be kind.

Several years ago, Robert Fulghum gave us a wonderful poem, the title of which countered all the collected wisdom of academia: "All I Really Need to Know I Learned in Kindergarten." It tackled the complexities of life in a few simple suggestions, like "Share everything, play fair, don't hit people."

Maybe we all need to go back and repeat kindergarten.

The Shakers were a religious community from England that moved to the United States in the mid-nineteenth century. They were known for, among other things, their simple style of living. Their handmade furniture continues to be coveted by many, largely due to its clean, austere design. One of their leaders, Elder Joseph Brackett, penned the song, "Simple Gifts" that has been performed by countless popular singers and orchestras. Its opening lines suggest a welcome contrast from the busy, complex, and cluttered lives most of us live:

"'Tis the gift to be simple, 'tis the gift to be free
'Tis the gift to come down where we ought to be."

I can't tell you where you ought to be, but I can assure that the gift of simplicity is one you will treasure once you find it. A good place to start is to create a list. I call it the "Not-to-Do List." What will you stop doing or say no to in order to free yourself from those things that enslave you? Simplicity is really a process of subtraction, removing things from your life rather than adding things. As Lao Tzu advises,

> Manifest plainness,
> Embrace simplicity,
> Reduce selfishness,
> Have few desires.

GRATITUDE

Here's a little experiment. Take a few minutes, and list all the things you don't have but would like to have. We'll call this the "life-sucks" list. Include things like a relationship that's been damaged or broken. Your biggest regrets. The year you got downsized. Anything thing that's lacking in your life.

Now shift gears, and begin making another list. I'll call it the "life-is-pretty-darn-good" list. Write down everything you can think of that's good in your life: the things that make you happy or give you great satisfaction. Maybe your kids. Your spouse. Your salary. Your last vacation.

OK, how did you feel as you worked on both lists? Chances are, as you looked at how your life sucked, you felt pretty lousy, but when you began listing all the pretty darn good things in your life, you felt a lot better.

What you felt as you worked on the second list was gratitude, a wonderful emotion that occurs when you focus on what you have as opposed to what you lack. Unfortunately, the overriding message of our consumerist culture is that you don't have enough—of anything. This might explain why so many people feel so lousy. According to the World Happiness Report (yes, there really is such a thing), Americans rank ninth in happiness, despite living in one of the richest countries in the world.

According to several studies by psychologists, gratitude leads to greater levels of happiness. In one study conducted by Dr. Martin E. P. Seligman, a psychologist at the University of Pennsylvania, participants were asked each week about their early memories. One assignment was to write and personally deliver a letter of gratitude to someone they had never thanked for something, and the participants' happiness scores went off the charts.[4]

Gratitude makes us happy because it reminds us how fortunate we are. I've read more than one hundred books on gratitude, and the general theme of most of these books is that gratitude leads to an attitude of abundance. It makes us aware that we have more than what we need, which is true of most of us in the developed world. It's just that we tend to focus on what we don't have. Often, some of the most grateful people I know are those who have very little. I believe they've learned that what little they have is a gift to be enjoyed and appreciated.

Because we are repeatedly told we need more, gratitude does not come naturally. We have to cultivate it. Here are a few ways to create an attitude of gratitude.

Create a gratitude journal. Take a few minutes during your lunch break or before you go to bed, and write down three good things in your life. Do it every day.

Say thank you. Make it a habit to say thank you whenever you can. Thank the person at the cash register for checking you

---

4 http://www.health.harvard.edu/healthbeat/giving-thanks-can-make-you-happier.

through. Thank your spouse for being faithful to you. Thank the kid who clears your table at the restaurant so that you don't have to.

Write thank-you notes. Put one in your child's lunch box. Send one to a public official in your city. Stick one in your mailbox addressed to "My wonderful mail carrier."

Stop and think. Consider what went into even the smallest pleasure you enjoy. Someone put the seed in the ground, watered it, and fertilized it, and someone else bent over, picked it, and carried it to a wagon. Then someone else washed and packed it, put it on a truck, and then someone else displayed it attractively—all so that you could enjoy that sweet, delicious strawberry you're eating.

Pray. I believe all good things come from God. I know, I know. You may not, and if that's the case, you can skip this one. By thanking God for all that I am blessed with, I am becoming more of a grateful person.

When we are grateful, we realize that we have everything we need and become immune to the message of more that hammers away at us. Sarah Ban Breathnach, author of the bestselling book *Simple Abundance*, writes about the life-changing dynamic of gratitude: "You simply will not be the same person two months from now after consciously giving thanks each day for the abundance that exists in your life. And you will have set in motion an ancient spiritual law: the more you have and are grateful for, the more will be given you." Gratitude creates a sense of peacefulness and contentment that allows us to truly enjoy life regardless of its circumstances. When I reach this state—and I don't always—resources and people just seem to show up in my life to help with the tasks at hand. I call it "God's economy," because you can never out give God.

◆ ◆ ◆

If you want to have an influence on others, practice humility, because in an increasingly self-absorbed culture, it is the humble individual who will shine as a beacon.

◆ ◆ ◆

Humor, humility, simplicity, and gratitude—four audibles to keep in your game plan and use as often as you need them. You can't crack jokes all the time, and let's face it—we're all on a learning curve when it comes to the other three audibles. But after further review, you'll discover that these four qualities will keep you going until the clock finally winds down.

Go to the Tape

1. Write three things down each day that you are grateful for.
2. Take five things out of your closet or drawers, and give them away. Make sure one item is meaningful to you.
3. Find something to laugh about each day—a real belly laugh.
4. Try to put others first before yourself each day.

CHAPTER 13

Postgame Reflection–the Final Ticks on the Clock

◆ ◆ ◆

All men die, but very few men live.

—William Wallace, "Guardian
of Scotland," *Braveheart*

Reflection is not just sitting around thinking big thoughts. It's not what they used to call "navel gazing," which the dictionary defines as "useless, excessive self-contemplation." The kind of reflection that I've been writing about always results in action. You reflect to gain understanding, and then you act on what you have learned. And the ultimate experience of reflection informs us that there is an expiration date on our lives; our lives, as we know it, will end.

"Gee thanks, Sweeney! Are you always this upbeat?"

Bear with me, because if you get this, you'll be one of the few, with reference to William Wallace quoted above, who will live. A lot of people are alive, but they are not really living. They get up, go to work, come home, turn on the TV, go to bed, get up, go to work, come home…Throw in a few weeks of vacation every year, the occasional celebrations of birthdays and weddings and anniversaries, and all of a sudden, you're approaching the finish line. It's like the guy who went to his twenty-fifth college reunion and later said to his wife, "I can't believe how fast my classmates got old." To which she wisely replied, "And they're saying the same thing about you, honey."

People often say time is money, but I say time is life itself. You can always make more money, but you can't make more time. You only have so many ticks on the clock left, and unlike football, there's no time clock winding down that you can see. In essence, you have no idea when the game is going to end. You have a choice, regardless of how much time you have left. You can play it safe and hope for the best, or you can stare the clock in the face and choose to live each day, each minute, each second to the fullest. Or as Steve Jobs once said, "Remembering you are going to die is the best way I know to avoid the trap of thinking you have something to lose."

◆ ◆ ◆

The ultimate experience of reflection informs us that there is an expiration date on our lives; our lives, as we know it, will end.

◆ ◆ ◆

Have you ever watched a football or basketball game in which a team got the lead and then tried to slow things down? Work the clock? Sometimes it's called "letting the air out of the ball." Most of the time it backfires. The team gets out of its rhythm and loses the game. Most of us live our lives the same way. We reach a point where everything seems to be going in the right direction, so we go on autopilot. We live as if we'll live forever, and that's why we tend to fall into the same routines and habits that characterize our lives. We're afraid to try new things or do anything extraordinary because we're opting for the familiar, the comfortable. It's called "getting in a rut," and I believe we're more vulnerable than we think.

◆ ◆ ◆

**Twenty years from now you will be more
disappointed by the things you didn't
do than by the ones you did do.
—H. Jackson Brown Jr.**

◆ ◆ ◆

Bronnie Ware is a nurse who specializes in palliative care. Her patients are given only weeks or months to live. Over the years, she recorded her experiences of caring for these people who had gone home to die, and the result was her book *The Top Five Regrets of the Dying: A Life Transformed by the Dearly Departing*. Part of that is motivated by our fear of dying. The title alone says something about the way we live—or don't live. Can you relate to any of these?

* I wish I'd had the courage to live a life true to myself, not the life others expected of me.
* I wish I hadn't worked so hard.
* I wish I had the courage to express my feelings.
* I wish I had stayed in touch with my friends.
* I wish that I had let myself be happier.

How sad to come to the end of your life with such regrets. According to author Shannon Alder, "When you settle for anything short of the best life God wants to offer you, then you have been tempted to remain safe, and the accountability for not changing your life becomes your prison of regret."

You can avoid those regrets by reflecting on the end of your journey. Doing so has little to do with dying. It's all about living. Here's the way I look at the time we have left. Let's start with the planet. It's about 4.6 billion years old, give or take a few centuries. We as humans have existed for roughly two-hundred thousand years. Each of us individually will live for approximately eighty years. Now, if you take the age of the planet and compress it into one day—twenty-four hours—and then compress our own life expectancy in the same ratio, those eighty years become a half a second. Assuming you're in the middle of your life, anywhere from forty to fifty years, you know how much longer you have in that compressed time? Less than a quarter of a second. It's not tragic that you only have a quarter of a second left on the clock. The real tragedy comes if you waste it. And a lot of us do. Even if you don't believe the earth is that old, the point still stands—time is precious.

If you can't get your arms around a quarter of a second, here's another way to think about the final ticks on the clock. Let's assume, just for the sake of argument, that we're going to live eighty-five years. That's 31,025 days. We sleep for ten thousand days. We work for about eleven thousand days and spend another seven hundred days commuting to and from work. The average person watches TV for 2,750 days! And not to be indelicate, but we spend another seven hundred days in the bathroom. That all adds up to 25,150 days, which leaves us with 5,875 days, *if* we live to be eighty-five.

I've lived for 20,805 days. If I live to be ninety—a guy can dream, right?—I've got 12,045 days left, minus the time I spend sleeping and going to the bathroom. I like to think of this as QTR—quality time remaining. When I think of the ticks on the clock this way, it motivates me to live out that quality time to the best of my ability and to make the most of every moment. It also helps me recognize that I really will never know exactly how many quality days I have left, so why not live today as if it were my last? As far as I'm concerned, once you reach the age of fifty, people should live by the philosophy of Andy Dufresne (Tim Robbins) from the movie *Shawshank Redemption*: "I guess it comes down to a simple choice really...Get busy living, or get busy dying."

You would think that as we run out of time, we would become almost frenetic about checking off the boxes on our bucket lists, but what I've observed is that the older we get, the fewer risks we take. We joke about rocking chairs and shuffleboard, but the reality is that a lot of people die before they die. They quit dreaming. And I'm not just talking about retirees. When was the last time you did something out of the ordinary? I mean something that was truly "out of character" for you? Henry David Thoreau was right when in he wrote in *Walden* that "The mass of men lead lives of quiet desperation." The gravity of the ordinary holds us down from the rare atmosphere of adventure that we crave. It's what finds us in our golden years woefully looking at a list of regrets instead of adding to a list of incredibly exhilarating experiences. I love the way the documentary filmmaker Nick Davies describes the way we move from youthful wonder at the possibilities ahead of us to settling for the ordinary:

> Once, the world was full of mysteries, some of them frightening, some of them wonderful, some of them merely fascinating. Now, it can be a banal and predictable place, the

tracks of daily life so well-beaten and defined, our culture awash with the imbecile obvious, our existence suffocating in safety. But mysteries remain.

Banal and predictable.

Remember a few years back when George H. W. Bush celebrated his ninetieth birthday with a parachute jump? Why should that be news? OK, ex-presidents get a lot of publicity. But the big deal wasn't that he was a former president; rather, it was that he was ninety. Why shouldn't *every* ninety-year-old jump out of an airplane? I mean, what have they got to lose? A few more ticks on the clock? Instead of fixating on the dangers and drawbacks of living life to the fullest even into your nineties, become inspired by what you have to gain. As the clock ticks down—which it does for all of us, regardless of your age—don't just dream about the things you wish you could do. Make them happen.

President Bush had every reason to play it safe and just eat cake on his birthday. Ninety-year-olds don't jump out of planes. He was confined to a wheelchair. A year earlier he spent several days in the hospital with a serious respiratory infection. He could break a leg, or worse. But if you saw the look on his face captured in a photograph from another jumper, you'd agree that he was embracing the invigorating reality that you're never too old to take a risk.

After further reflection, I decided that's how I wanted to live my life. Every day. I want my life to expand with each day rather than watch it get smaller and shrunken. That's why I say the ultimate value of reflection is the recognition that you only have so much time left, and the action required of this reflection is answering these questions: What are you going to do about it? How are you going to spend it?

◆ ◆ ◆

What if you turned the tables and someday became today? What would your life look like if instead of always looking forward to someday, you turned those somedays into today?

◆ ◆ ◆

To help you find the best answers to those questions, I'd like you to think in terms of today versus someday. Have you ever sat back and said "someday I'm going to..."? I've provided some examples below.

- Someday I'm going to take that dream vacation with my family to Italy.
- Someday I'm going to start doing a date night with my spouse.
- Someday I'm going to run a marathon.
- Someday I am going to get my finances in order and start saving money.
- Someday I'm going to call that friend who hurt me and tell her, "It's OK. I forgive you."
- Someday I'm going to make out my will.
- Someday I'm going to join a gym and lose thirty pounds.
- Someday I'm going to go on that mission trip with my church and help build a school for children in Guatemala.
- Someday I'm going to learn a second language.
- Someday I'm going to write that book that's been bubbling up inside of me.
- Someday I'm going to build a treehouse for my grandchildren.
- Someday I'm going to get more spiritually centered.

If you really want to get the most out of the time you have left on this planet, stop reading, and take a few minutes right now to make a list of three "somedays." Three out-of-the ordinary things you hope to do someday. They could be anything, from something big and audacious that seems almost impossible, to a small act of kindness or appreciation. Don't think of anything else. Three things—if you don't do them, then you'll die with regrets. Write them down:

1. _____
2. _____
3. _____

After you write down these three someday goals, I'd like you to review what you did today. If you're like most people, it probably looks something like this:

* Woke up, grabbed your iPhone to check your e-mail and Facebook page to see what your friends are up to
* Took a shower, ate breakfast
* Drove the kids to school, then on to work
* Logged into your computer and once again took a quick peek at your Facebook page to see that your brother's kid got the lead in the school musical, and another friend posted family pictures of a Disney cruise—lucky stiffs!
* Went to a couple of meetings, then it was time for lunch
* Back at your desk to try to finish that project that your boss has been waiting for
* Left work, picked the kids up, made dinner
* Picked up that book you've been meaning to read, slumped into your La-Z-Boy, and for some reason turned on the TV—just too tired to read

* Laughed a lot—those comedies sure are funny!
* Looked for your spouse so that you could finally decide where to go on vacation this year, but he/she had already gone to bed
* Poured a glass of wine and headed back to the La-Z-Boy, this time picking up the latest issue of *People* magazine—those celebrities sure are living the good life!
* Went to bed

There's absolutely nothing wrong with any of the activities I just listed. We all do them or activities similar to them. But as you review how you spent today, ask yourself, "What one thing did I do that gets me closer to achieving any of the three someday goals I listed above?" As I pointed out at the beginning of this chapter, reflection is useless if it doesn't produce action. You can reflect on someday all day long—a lot of people do—but if that's all you do, you're just daydreaming.

But what if you turned the tables and someday became today? What would your life look like if instead of always looking forward to someday, you turned those somedays into today?

I began this book describing the best year of my life. I hope it didn't sound like I was bragging. My intention was to cast a vision for you, to get you thinking, "How could I experience a richer, fuller, more meaningful life?" And not just this year, but every year you have left on this planet. And I believe it's possible, but it won't happen by thinking about it, hoping for it, or waiting for it to happen.

One of my favorite musicals is *The Music Man,* and one of my favorite scenes is when Professor Harold Hill, a sort of snake-oil salesman who falls head over heels for Marian, the librarian, in the small town of River City, Iowa, asks her to meet him at the footbridge in fifteen minutes. She responds, "Oh, not tonight. Maybe tomorrow." Undaunted, he presses on. "Oh, my dear little librarian. You pile up enough tomorrows, and you'll find you are left with nothing but a lot of empty yesterdays. I don't know about you, but I'd like to make today worth remembering."

I'm with the professor. I want every day ahead of me to count, and I've been trying to make that happen. It all started with looking at my someday list and figuring out a way to turn those somedays into today. Go back to your list of three somedays. Transfer them to an index card or your cell phone and carry them around with you. When you wake up tomorrow morning, before you step out of bed, look at your somedays and ask yourself, "What can I do today that will help turn one of these three somedays into today?" Whatever your answer is, commit yourself to doing it. Not tomorrow. Today. Before you crawl back into bed.

If you do that every day, it won't be long before those three somedays actually happen. That's when you start a new list. That's when you become one of the few who live.

Yes, we all have an expiration date. You can ignore that reality and keep living for someday, or you can embrace it and discover how to truly live. Today. And it begins with reflection—giving yourself the gift of time and silence to listen. According to Thomas Merton, the Catholic writer and Trappist monk, reflection will promise you two things:

In the silence, you will find God, and in the silence, you will find yourself. These will be the two greatest discoveries of your life. But these discoveries will not be moments of epiphany; they will be gradual. You will discover a little at a time, something like a jigsaw puzzle being put together. I cannot imagine how miserable life would be without the adventure of discovering God and self. It is this process of discovery that allows us to make sense of life.

Welcome to the adventure.

CHAPTER 14

Putting It All Together— After Further Review

◆ ◆ ◆

WHENEVER I TALK TO PEOPLE about the power of reflection, a common response is, "Does it really work?" That's a legitimate question, and I usually answer by saying, "It depends." Reflection will not solve all your problems. It will not inoculate you from the day-to-day realities of life on this planet. It won't guarantee financial success, take two inches off your waistline, or grow hair on that bald spot. As a culture, we've been conditioned to think that there's a pill or secret formula to deliver whatever we desire. Reflection won't do that, but it will do so much more.

When you reflect more, you will get clear, get free, and get going in your life. You will begin to discover (or rediscover) things that have lain dormant in you that will lead to greater meaning, purpose, and joy. It may not give you the *things* you've always wanted, but it will give you the life you always wanted. Here is what you will discover when you go to the sidelines, look into that little monitor, and review how you're playing the game:

1. You realize that life is not all about you, and that you are not the center of the universe.

2. You will discover that you belong to something much bigger than yourself.

3. You will learn that if you help others get what *they* want, you will get *everything* you want in life—and more.

4. You will become grateful for everything in your life when you understand that both the good and the bad are blessings to receive with humility and joy.

5. You will begin to ask yourself, "How much is enough?" which reveals the liberating truth that less is more.

6. You will become humble, without feeling that you have lost anything. Others can have more, look better, be right more often, and win more, and it's OK.

7. You will eradicate hurry from your life. Life slows down, but in a good way. As you become less busy, you will become more focused and accomplish more of what truly matters to you.

8. You will experience peace of the mind and of the soul. Anxiety will become a distant memory.

9. You will experience fulfillment and satisfaction because you will know that whatever you want in your life is either here or on its way.

10. You begin to detach yourself from outcomes. Bad things will happen—they always do—but you see them from a new, eternal perspective. In other words, you will not freak out when stocks plummet.

11. You will be able to recognize the counterfeits, knowing what is real and what is not, who is real and who is not.

12. You will know and value joy as you learn that happiness is fickle and fleeting. Joy is an attitude that can permeate your soul.

13. You will become more aware of your thoughts and feelings as the numbness of life fades away.

14. You will recognize when you veer off course and will be able to get back on track more quickly because you understand that you're not perfect, and therefore you won't have to deceive yourself anymore.

15. You will learn how to measure your life to discover what it would look like if it really turned out great.

16. You will benefit from the counsel of your senior partners, role models, and guides, who help you on your journey because they are always there and always available.

17. You will see God in every encounter and recognize that He is guiding you, even if you don't understand how that happens. He believes in you!

18. You will realize that there is a season for everything in life, which gives you the freedom to enjoy the moment.

19. You laugh more, especially at yourself, because life is full of punchlines.

20. You will ask more questions instead of trying to have all the answers, and you will understand that the two most important questions before you are "Who am I?" and "Why am I here?"

21. You will discover that everything in this world is energy and that your goal is to tap into this divine energy more frequently and for longer periods of time.

22. You will begin to live your legacy by leaving every situation and person you encounter better than when you found it.

23. You will accept the reality that your life lasts for a half a second, which gives you the courage to not waste a nanosecond.

24. You will learn the fine art of letting go and practice it every day.
25. You will turn all of your somedays into today.

After further review, all of this can happen to you.

RECOMMENDED READING LIST

◆ ◆ ◆

Abraham, Joe. *Entrepreneurial DNA: The Breakthrough Discovery That Aligns Your Business to Your Unique Strengths.*

Attwood, Janet, and Chris Attwood. *The Passion Test: The Effortless Path to Discovering Your Life Purpose.*

Buettner, Dan. *The Blue Zones, Second Edition: 9 Lessons for Living Longer from the People Who've Lived the Longest.*

Buford, Bob. *Halftime.*

Buford, Bob, and Ken Blanchard. *Finishing Well: The Adventure of Life beyond Halftime.*

Buford, Bob, and Peter Drucker. *Stuck in Halftime.*

Butterworth, Eric, and David F. Miller. *Spiritual Economics: The Principles and Process of True Prosperity.*

Calloway, Joe. *Be the Best at What Matters Most: The Only Strategy You Will Ever Need.*

Campbell, Joseph. *The Hero with a Thousand Faces.*

Campbell, Joseph, and Bill Moyers. *The Power of Myth.*

Campbell, Joseph, and Diane K. Osbon. *Reflections on the Art of Living: A Joseph Campbell Companion.*

Campbell, Joseph, and Phil Cousineau. *The Hero's Journey: Joseph Campbell on His Life and Work.*

Canfield, Jack, and Janet Switzer. *The Success Principles: How to Get from Where You Are to Where You Want to Be.*

Carnegie, Dale. *How to Win Friends & Influence People.*

Chapman, Gary. *The 5 Love Languages: The Secret to Love That Lasts.*

Christensen, Clayton M., and James Allworth. *How Will You Measure Your Life?*

Collins, Jim. *Good to Great: Why Some Companies Make the Leap and Others Don't.*

Covey, Stephen R. *The 7 Habits of Highly Effective People: Powerful Lessons in Personal Change.*

Crowley, Chris, and Henry S. Lodge. *Younger Next Year: Live Strong, Fit, and Sexy—Until You're 80 and Beyond.*

Duckworth, Angela. *Grit: The Power of Passion and Perseverance.*

Duhigg, Charles. *The Power of Habit: Why We Do What We Do in Life and Business.*

Dychtwald, Ken, and Daniel J. Kadlec. *A New Purpose: Redefining Money, Family, Work, Retirement, and Success.*

Dyer, Wayne. *Excuses Begone! How to Change Lifelong, Self-Defeating Thinking Habits.*

—————. *Wishes Fulfilled: Mastering the Art of Manifesting.*

—————. *Being in Balance: 9 Principles for Creating Habits to Match Your Desires.*

—————. *The Power of Intention.*

—————. *Manifest Your Destiny: The Nine Spiritual Principles for Getting Everything You Want.*

Emery, Stewart, and Mark Thompson. *Success Built to Last: Creating a Life That Matters.*

Frankl, Viktor E., and William J. Winslade. *Man's Search for Meaning.*

Gladwell, Malcolm. *David and Goliath: Underdogs, Misfits, and the Art of Battling Giants.*

Goddard, Neville. *The Power of Awareness.*

Goodwin, Doris Kearns. *Team of Rivals: The Political Genius of Abraham Lincoln.*

Hicks, Esther, and Jerry Hicks. *Ask and It Is Given: Learning to Manifest Your Desires.*

Hill, Napoleon. *Think and Grow Rich.*

Jung, Carl, and Aniela Jaffe. *Memories, Dreams, Reflections.*

Kelly, Matthew. *The Rhythm of Life: Living Every Day with Passion and Purpose.*

Kraemer, Harry M. *From Values to Action: The Four Principles of Values-Based Leadership.*

Krauthammer, Charles. *Things That Matter.*

Levinson, Daniel. *The Seasons of a Man's Life.*

Lowney, Chris. *Heroic Living: Discover Your Purpose and Change the World.*

————. *Heroic Leadership: Best Practices from a 450-Year-Old Company That Changed the World.*

Mackay, Harvey B. *Swim with the Sharks without Being Eaten Alive: Outsell, Outmanage, Outmotivate, and Outnegotiate Your Competition.*

Martin, James, SJ. *The Jesuit Guide to (Almost) Everything: A Spirituality for Real Life.*

Maslow, Abraham. *Toward a Psychology of Being.*

Maxwell, John C., and Steven R. Covey. *The 21 Irrefutable Laws of Leadership: Follow Them and People Will Follow You.*

McKeown, Greg. *Essentialism: The Disciplined Pursuit of Less.*

Merton, Thomas. *The Seven Storey Mountain.*

Murphy, Joseph. *The Power of Your Subconscious Mind.*

Myss, Caroline. *Sacred Contracts: Awakening Your Divine Potential.*

Newport, Cal. *So Good They Can't Ignore You: Why Skills Trump Passion in the Quest for Work You Love.*

Pink, Daniel H. *Drive: The Surprising Truth about What Motivates Us.*

Rath, Tom. *Eat Move Sleep: How Small Choices Lead to Big Changes.*

–––––. *StrengthsFinder 2.0.*

Reagan, Ronald. *The Great Communicator.*

Reeb, Lloyd. *From Success to Significance: When the Pursuit of Success Isn't Enough.*

Rohr, Richard. *Breathing under Water: Spirituality and the Twelve Steps.*

–––––. *Falling upward: A Spirituality for the Two Halves of Life.*

–––––. *The Art of Letting Go: Living the Wisdom of Saint Francis.*

—————. *Immortal Diamond: The Search for Our True Self.*

—————. *The Naked Now: Learning to See as the Mystics See.*

Sheehy, Gail. *Passages: Predictable Crises of Adult Life.*

Sinek, Simon. *Start with Why: How Great Leaders Inspire Everyone to Take Action.*

Sweeney, Joe, and Mike Yorkey. *Networking Is a Contact Sport: How Staying Connected and Serving Others Will Help You Grow Your Business, Expand Your Influence—or Even Land Your Next Job.*

—————. *Moving the Needle: Get Clear, Get Free, and Get Going in Your Career, Business, and Life.*

Tolle, Eckhart. *The Power of Now: A Guide to Spiritual Enlightenment.*

Warren, Rick. *The Purpose Driven Life: What on Earth Am I Here For?*

Willink, Jocko, and Leif Babin. *Extreme Ownership: How US Navy SEALs Lead and Win.*

ABOUT THE AUTHOR

◆ ◆ ◆

Joe Sweeney has spent thirty-plus years blending his love of business and passion for sports. He has owned, operated, and sold four manufacturing companies, headed up the Wisconsin Sports Authority, and launched a sports marketing firm. Joe purchased equity interest in an investment banking firm and served as president and managing director. He is now an accomplished author, internationally-known speaker, and investor in private equity companies.

Joe's passion is studying human behavior. He has used the fields of sports, business, and military as his laboratory to better understand why certain people outperform others. Joe has served on twenty-eight boards of directors and is currently active on six.

Joe received his BA from Saint Mary's University of Minnesota and his MBA from the University of Notre Dame.

The author of *After Further Review, Moving the Needle,* and *New York Times* bestseller *Networking Is a Contact Sport* resides in Milwaukee, Wisconsin.

CONNECT WITH JOE:

Joe Sweeney is a dynamic speaker, coach, and trainer who encourages and educates others about what it means to excel in today's business climate as well as how networking can grow your business, expand your influence, and make life richer and more meaningful.

Contact Joe at www.joesweeney.com to find out more about hiring him to guide you and your team to create fulfilling life experiences and inspire you to move the needle in your career business and life.

Download a free copy of the After Further Review Journal which includes all of the "*Go to the Tape*" questions shared at the end of each chapter. Access here: www.joesweeney.com/AFRJournal

◆ ◆ ◆

NETWORKING IS A CONTACT SPORT

WHEN JOE SWEENEY WROTE HIS *New York Times* bestseller, *Networking Is a Contact Sport*, his goal was simple: help others benefit from all he has learned about building rewarding relationships and successful businesses.

For more than thirty years, Joe has traveled the world asking questions, giving of himself, and doing his best to discover what motivates people. And now you have an opportunity to learn the simple skills Joe has perfected to grow your business, expand your influence, and take both your professional and personal success to the next level.

MOVING THE NEEDLE

Through his second book, *Moving the Needle: Get Clear, Get Free, and Get Going in Your Career, Business, and Life,* and his training program, the *Winning Game Plan,* Joe will show you how to put action plans into place, become accountable, and ultimately, achieve your goals. If you've been hoping to gain much-needed traction at work and in your personal life, then Joe Sweeney will show you how to move forward.

Made in the USA
Columbia, SC
27 January 2020